LUCENT LIBRARY *of* HISTORICAL ERAS

PEOPLE OF THE NILE: RHYTHMS OF DAILY LIFE

DON NARDO

LUCENT BOOKS

An imprint of Thomson Gale, a part of The Thomson Corporation

THOMSON

GALE

Detroit • New York • San Francisco • San Diego • New Haven, Conn. • Waterville, Maine • London • Munich

THOMSON

GALE

LIBRARY OF CONGRESS CATALOGING-IN-PUBLICATION DATA

Nardo, Don, 1947–
  People of the Nile : rhythms of daily life / by Don Nardo.
     p. cm. — (Lucent library of historical eras)
  Includes bibliographical references and index.
  ISBN 1-59018-705-9 (hardcover : alk. paper)
  1. Egypt—Social life and customs—To 332 B.C.—Juvenile literature. I. Title. II.
Series: Lucent library of historical eras. Ancient Egypt
DT61.N3278 2005
932—dc22

                                                                        2005001306

Printed in the United States of America

Contents

◆

Foreword

Looking back from the vantage point of the present, history can be viewed as a myriad of intertwining roads paved by human events. Some paths stand out—broad highways whose mileposts, even from a distance of centuries, are clear. The events that propelled the rise to power of Germany's Third Reich, its role in World War II, and its eventual demise, for example, are well defined and documented.

Other roads are less distinct, their route sometimes hidden from view. Modern legislatures may have developed from old tribal councils, for example, but the links between them are indistinct in places, open to discussion and interpretation.

The architecture of civilization—law, religion, art, science, and government—as well as the more everyday aspects of our culture—what we eat, what we wear—all developed along the historical roads and byways. In that progression can be traced every facet of modern life.

A broad look back along these roads reveals that many paths—though of vastly different character—seem to converge at a few critical junctions. These intersections are those great historical eras that echo over the long, steady course of human history, extending beyond the past and into the present.

These epic periods of time are the focus of Lucent's Library of Historical Eras. They shine through the mists of history like beacons, illuminated by a burst of creativity that propels events forward—so bright that we, from thousands of years away, can clearly see the chain of events leading to the present.

Each Lucent Library of Historical Eras consists of a set of books that highlight various aspects of these major eras. For example, the Elizabethan England library features volumes on Queen Elizabeth I and her court, Elizabethan theater, the great playwrights, and everyday life in Elizabethan London.

The mini-library approach allows for the division of each era into its most significant and most interesting parts and the exploration of those parts in depth. Also, social and cultural trends as well as illustrative documents and eyewitness accounts can be prominently featured in individual volumes.

Lucent's Library of Historical Eras presents a wealth of information to young readers. The lively narrative, fully documented primary and secondary source quotations, maps, photographs, sidebars, and annotated bibliographies serve as launching points for class discussion and further research.

In studying the great historical eras, students also develop a better understanding of our own times. What we learn from the past and how we apply it in the present may shape the future and may determine whether our era will be a guiding light to those traveling future roads.

THE ANCIENT EGYPTIANS ENJOYED LIFE

Modern experts on ancient Egypt have changed their opinion rather dramatically in the past century about how much the Egyptians enjoyed life. Many early modern scholars noted that the Egyptians followed rigid social and other traditions and were resistant to change. And a majority of them were poor and lived in squalid conditions. Also, they were very religiously devout and obsessed with death and the afterlife. From this, a number of experts concluded that the Egyptians must have been a somber, serious, cheerless, even downtrodden people.

"Spend Your Days Joyfully"

However, this view—that the Egyptians' general outlook on life was essentially joyless—turned out to be wrong. "In surveying the evidence that survives from antiquity [ancient times]," Brooklyn Museum scholar James F. Romano writes, "we are left with the overall impression that most Egyptians loved life and were willing to overlook its hardships. Indeed, [to them]the perfect afterlife was merely an ideal version of their earthly existence."[1]

The evidence Romano mentions consists of several surviving writings attesting to a generally positive, optimistic outlook on life. Apparently the Egyptians recognized an age-old maxim that today is most often stated as "all work and no play makes Jack a dull boy." For example, a high royal administrator named Ptahhotep, who lived around 2400 B.C. (some forty-four hundred years ago), left behind some wise sayings that include these words:

Follow your heart [enjoy life]as long as you live. Do no more [work]than is required. Do not shorten the time of "follow-the-heart" [i.e., leisure time]. Trimming its moments offends the soul. Don't waste time on daily cares, beyond providing for your household. When wealth has come, follow your heart. Wealth does no good [i.e., cannot buy happiness] if one is glum![2]

A similar sentiment was found in the tomb of a pharaoh who reigned shortly before 2000 B.C.:

Let your heart be strong. Let [worries and cares] fade from your thoughts. Look to yourself and follow your heart's desire while you live. . . . Let not your heart be troubled that the day of mourning for you must come. . . . So spend your days joyfully and do not be weary with living![3]

Obviously most ancient Egyptians worked long hours and could not spend all of their time "joyfully," as the writer of the tomb inscription advised. Yet strong evidence suggests that, like most people today, they managed to find some time for leisure and play. And they combined work and play the best way they could, achieving a satisfying balance between the two. Members of both the upper and the lower classes enjoyed and participated in numerous sports and games, for instance. These included hunting, fishing, swimming and other water sports, board games, ball games, running contests, and many more. Overall, says Romano, they were "a fun-loving people who filled their leisure hours with pleasant diversions."[4]

The Written Sources

How do scholars and other modern observers know about such diversions, as well as about the daily work, duties, beliefs, and living conditions of a people who vanished so long ago? For the most part, the evidence for how the ancient Egyptians lived comes from two general categories of sources. First are the written ones, which also break down into two general groups. The first group of written sources consists of the surviving accounts from the Egyptians themselves.

On the plus side, these surviving writings are numerous. This is because a great

A surviving ostrakon bears part of an ancient Egyptian text.

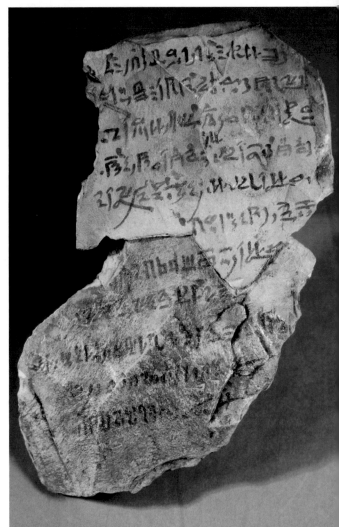

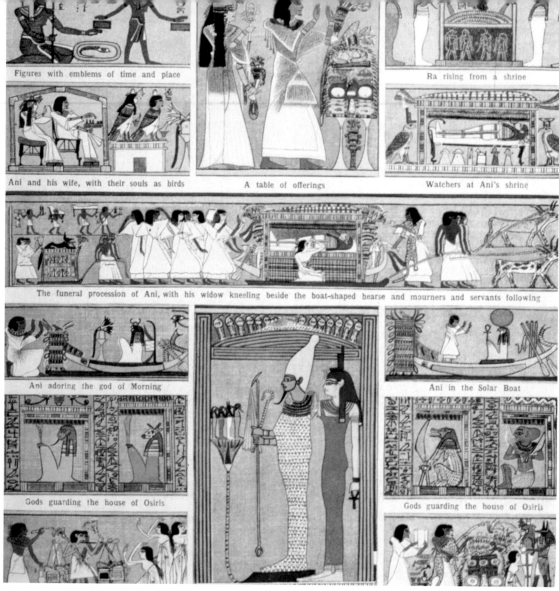

Figures with emblems of time and place

Ra rising from a shrine

Ani and his wife, with their souls as birds

A table of offerings

Watchers at Ani's shrine

The funeral procession of Ani, with his widow kneeling beside the boat-shaped hearse and mourners and servants following

Ani adoring the god of Morning

Ani in the Solar Boat

Gods guarding the house of Osiris

Gods guarding the house of Osiris

Paintings dealing with Egyptian life and death rituals highlight the Ani Papyrus. Missing is commentary on people's personal thoughts and feelings.

many of them were made on stone, ostra-ka (pieces of broken pottery), and papyri (documents written on papyrus, a kind of paper made from a water plant). Stone and pottery are hard and long lasting; and Egypt's largely arid climate and dry sands have preserved large numbers of ancient papyri that would have rotted away to dust in more humid climates.

On the minus side, however, the vast majority of these surviving writings do not reveal very much about people's private lives and thoughts. As noted Egyptologist Gay Robins points out:

The Egyptians did not develop a tradition of expressing personal opinions or of self-examination in their writing. Letters do not comment on political or other events. They do not give accounts of the writer's daily life, descriptions of travels, or observations of what is going on around them. Nothing like a personal notebook or diary has ever been found. Neither men nor women jotted down their thoughts or a record of events at the end of the day before lying down to sleep. Thus, we seldom encounter individual personality in Egypt because the Egyptians do not seem to have been concerned with perpetuating themselves as they actually were, but only as they conformed to society's ideals.[5]

Ptahhotep's sayings and many other similar extant documents are a case in point. They state much about the ideal way a person *should* live, but little about how the authors and their neighbors actually *did* live. Fortunately, within those ancient statements of ideals one can sometimes read between the lines. In his eighteenth maxim, for instance, Ptahhotep says, "If you want friendship to endure in the house you enter . . . beware of approaching the [family]women! Unhappy is the place where it is done, [and]unwelcome is he who intrudes on them."[6] In warning that it is improper for a guest to socialize or flirt with the women in someone else's house, the author reveals certain accepted customs surrounding home life and the treatment of women.

Also fortunate for modern observers is the fact that a number of hymns and love songs have survived from ancient Egypt. Some, like the one excerpted here, are startlingly vivid and employ deft and beautiful imagery: "Love of you is mixed deep in my vitals, like water stirred into flour for bread . . . like pastry and honey mixed to perfection."[7] Along with the evidence for sports and games, these songs further demonstrate that the Egyptians were a passionate, expressive people, certainly no less so than people today.

A second group of surviving written accounts about ancient Egyptian life comes from Greek and Roman writers who visited or lived in Egypt in the late first millennium B.C. and early first millennium A.D. (In that era, the country, no longer an independent nation, was ruled by Greeks and Romans.) Of particular importance are the Greek historians Herodotus (fifth century B.C.) and Diodorus Siculus (first century B.C.). Both visited Egypt for extended periods and recorded much valuable information about the people and their customs. Somewhat later, the Romans Pliny the Elder and Seneca the Younger (both first century A.D.) jotted down still more interesting facts about the Egyptians. (Seneca actually kept a house in Egypt.)

Physical Evidence and Historical Context

Supplementing these written accounts are discoveries made by archaeologists, scholars who specialize in digging up and studying the artifacts of past cultures.

Their efforts continue. And each year excavations reveal new papyri, houses, gravesites, tools, pottery, coins, figurines, personal belongings, and other items that shed light on everyday life in Egypt.

Especially valuable are the remains of workers' villages, which were erected near large building sites and sometimes remained intact for two or more generations. Probably the best known and most revealing of these is at Deir el-Medina, on the Nile's west bank across the river from the ancient Egyptian capital of Thebes. A similar village began to come to light in the 1990s near the great pyramids on the Giza plateau (near modern Cairo). The remains of these and other workers' villages show the size and layout of the houses, the foods eaten by those who lived in them, their burial customs, and other important information.

In examining such evidence, archaeologists are always careful to put their find-

The ruins of Deir el-Medina, near ancient Thebes, have yielded valuable information about the everyday lives of average Egyptians.

ings in a historical context. Egyptian civilization thrived for several thousand years. During those many centuries, despite the strong emphasis the people placed on tradition, some customs, habits, beliefs, and artistic and literary styles underwent change. Burial practices among members of Egypt's wealthy and noble classes were not the same in the time of Christ as in the era of the first pharaohs, for example.

To make the job of studying those times easier, modern scholars have broken Egypt's ancient history into convenient periods and eras (which the Egyptians themselves did not recognize). First was the Old Kingdom (ca. 2686–2181 B.C.), during which most of Egypt's pyramids were built. Second was the Middle Kingdom (ca. 2055–1650 B.C.), in which Egypt began expanding its wealth through far-ranging trade. Third was the New Kingdom (ca. 1550–1069 B.C.), in which a series of strong pharaohs created an Egyptian empire. Scholars place several other periods before, between, and after these big three. Of particular importance are the Late Period (ca. 747–332 B.C.), during most of which members of various foreign-born families ruled Egypt; the Greek, or Ptolemaic, Period (323–30 B.C.), in which Greek rulers held sway in Egypt; and the Roman Period (30 B.C.–A.D. 395), in which a series of Roman emperors had control of the country.

Despite the social and material changes wrought during these long ages, most change occurred among the wealthy and middle classes, whose members could afford to adopt and adapt to new ideas, habits, and conveniences. As has been true

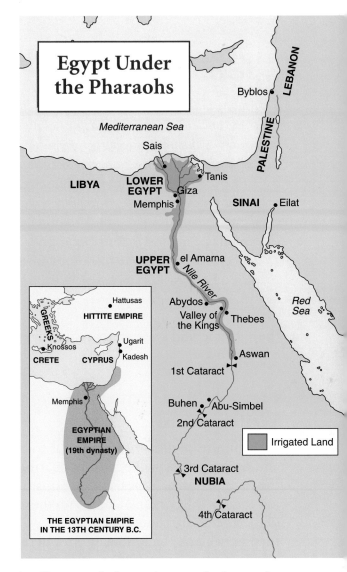

in all ages and places, the poor had to make do with very little and tended to fall back on traditional, very basic tools, customs, and habits. Usually ignored by richer folk and seldom described in contemporary writings, they and their homes and belongings most often disappeared, leaving few traces in the historical record. That makes archaeologists and other scholars try all

Seize the Day!

Among many surviving tomb inscriptions from ancient Egypt are harpers' songs, which, as the name suggests, were sung to the accompaniment of a harp. Often they reflected on the meaning of life and urged people to do their best to seek happiness during their short stay on earth. This example (translated by John L. Foster in his collection of ancient Egyptian literature) comes from a late New Kingdom tomb.

Seize the Day! Hold holiday! Be unwearied, unceasing, alive. . . . Let not your heart be troubled during your sojourn on earth, but seize the day as it passes! . . . Grieve not in your heart, whatever comes. Let sweet music play before you. Recall not the evil, loathsome [things]to Gods, but have joy, joy, joy, and pleasure! . . . Let your heart be drunk on the gift of [life]until that day comes when you [leave life].

the harder to find evidence that sheds light on their lives.

Eternal Life Through the Written Word

In the future, perhaps more papyrus rolls and other records will be found bearing the names, deeds, hopes, and dreams of less fortunate Egyptians, along with those of their better-off countrymen. If so, it will further validate the following prophetic words, written circa 1200 B.C. by one of the residents of the Deir el-Medina workers' village. Though peculiarly Egyptian in its preoccupation with eternal life, the statement remains a kernel of wisdom that rings true for people in all times and places:

> [The great buildings of the people of long ago are]now fallen . . . their headstones undiscovered in the dirt, their very graves forgotten. But their fame lives on in their papyrus rolls composed while they were still alive. And the memory of those who write such books [and of those they describe]shall last to the end of time and for eternity.[8]

Chapter One

The Focus of Life: Home and Family

As has been the case in nearly all human cultures, ancient or modern, the central focus of everyday life in ancient Egypt was the home and family. Evidence shows that the most common type of family unit was nuclear—consisting of a father, a mother, and their children. However, a fair proportion of Egyptian families also included grandparents, uncles, aunts, cousins, and/or in-laws sharing the same living space. In addition, some families had servants or slaves, who were often treated as extended family members. Therefore, whereas some families were relatively small, others were quite large.

Similarly, the size, layout, facilities, and luxuries of the houses in which these families dwelled varied widely. Social status and family income were obviously important factors in determining the size and quality of one's house. As is true in all societies, poor farmers, craftsmen, and laborers could afford only the most basic living quarters. These modest dwellings were the most common in Egypt because poor folk constituted the majority of the population. Members of a small middle class—made up of midlevel government administrators, scribes, army officers, priests, and a few rich merchants—could afford larger, more comfortable homes.

Not surprisingly, the biggest and most luxurious houses in Egypt belonged to members of the upper classes. Including royalty, nobles, army generals, and chief priests, they made up a small minority of the population—probably no more than 7 percent at any given time. But most of the country's wealth was concentrated in their houses, which were true mansions, and their families' possessions.

Upper-Class Houses

In fact, a typical upper-class townhouse (city dwelling) was a large two-story structure having dozens of rooms that served a wide variety of functions. Most often the

This wall painting shows servants, storage jars, fruits trees, and other aspects of everyday life in a well-to-do Egyptian country house.

rooms on the ground floor had utilitarian, or practical, uses. The kitchen and baking facilities were on the first story, for instance, along with workshops for craftsmen employed by the family, stalls for cattle and other animals, and extensive storerooms. The ground floor also featured one or more meeting rooms where the well-to-do owner greeted his guests and/or conducted business deals.

The more private living spaces were upstairs. Often the most central of these was the dining area, which connected to the kitchen downstairs via a stairway. The owner's bedroom was the largest of the sleeping chambers, which varied in number according to the size of the family. The stairway also led to the roof. It was usually flat and featured storage areas for fuel (wood and charcoal), servants' quarters, and a patio for enjoying the cool evening breezes.

Not all rich homes followed this plan, as there was a great deal of variety in the layout of Egyptian houses. About a dozen mansions featuring central courtyards were discovered at Illahun, in the Faiyum (a fertile region situated about thirty-five miles west of modern Cairo) in the 1890s. Presumably the owners were senior government officials and royal courtiers. In each of these homes the rectangular courtyard, which was open to the elements, was the nucleus of a large complex of up to sixty or seventy rooms. Kitchens, meeting rooms, and storerooms lined the courtyard, and corridors led away to bedrooms, women's quarters, servants' quarters, and so forth.

Still another kind of mansion was a kind of country villa (although it might be located in a city) surrounded by a tall masonry enclosure wall. This has come to be called the Amarna-villa type, after an ancient Egyptian city that modern scholars call el-Amarna (about 160 miles south of Cairo). Passing through a gate in the outer wall, one entered extensive grounds featuring gardens, well-trimmed trees and bushes, and sometimes artificial ponds stocked with fish. Around the edge of the garden were small structures that housed workshops, kitchens, stables, barns, and granaries. These and other facilities made a wealthy person's home an economic unit that could more or less survive on its own. Beyond the pleasant gardens stood the main house, which one entered via a flight of steps flanked by elegant stone columns. The first chamber beyond the front door was a small foyer. Then came a reception hall, with white stucco walls decorated with

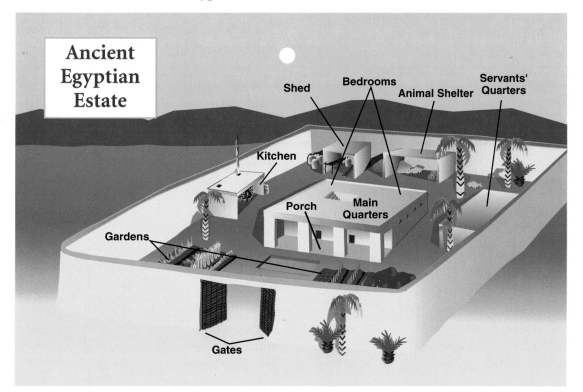

Ancient Egyptian Estate

Shed
Bedrooms
Animal Shelter
Servants' Quarters
Kitchen
Porch
Main Quarters
Gardens
Gates

animal, floral, or geometric patterns. The floor was covered with stone tiles and there was a large fireplace. On the far side of the reception hall one came to a square hall with a high roof supported by tall columns.

As in the case of the mansions with courtyards, doors in the perimeter of this tall, square hall led away to a host of rooms. The master's room usually featured an

Light and Heat in an Egyptian Home

Heating and lighting in ancient Egyptian houses were quite primitive compared to the situation in even the poorest of modern homes. For artificial light, the residents of an Egyptian house relied mainly on lamps that burned oil derived from palms, olives, or other plants. The simplest kind of oil lamp was a small bowl of oil in which the wick floated on the oil's surface. In better homes, more elaborate oil lamps rested atop tall stands. Candles made from animal fat and torches were also employed to light the interiors and exteriors of buildings at night. Heat for houses came mainly from brick or stone hearths that burned wood or charcoal. When possible, holes were punched in the roof to allow smoke to exit; but a good deal of smoke circulated inside living spaces, making the air pungent and, after long-term exposure, unhealthy.

extra-thick wall on the chamber's south side. The bed, consisting of a wooden frame with a mattress made from interwoven reeds and folded linen, was recessed into this insulating wall. This kept both outside noises and summer heat to a minimum. Instead of a pillow, most Egyptians laid their heads on wooden headrests that were curved to accommodate the neck. (For extra comfort, they sometimes lined the wood with layers of linen.) In addition to beds, the furniture in such homes included finely made wooden chairs, couches, stools, and chests for storage.

There were also small bathrooms connected to the bedrooms, although these were primitive compared to modern versions. There was no plumbing to speak of, for instance. Beneath the hole in the toilet seat sat a bucket partially filled with sand, which servants periodically carried away and emptied. And in the absence of bathtubs, the bather stood or sat in the center of the room and allowed a servant to pour water over him or her. (The dirty water usually drained away to the gardens through a narrow stone trough built into the floor.)

Poorer Houses

It appears that bathrooms were for the most part a luxury of the well-to-do, although a few middle-class homes did have them. The vast majority of Egyptians simply went to a private corner of their house, relieved themselves into a pottery container, and emptied it outside. They did not relieve themselves outside, as people

The houses in the workers' village at Deir el-Medina were constructed of a combination of mud bricks, fieldstones, and wood.

in many other ancient cultures did. This was confirmed by a comment made by the Greek historian Herodotus after his visit to Egypt in the fifth century B.C.: "Women pass water [urinate] standing up, men sitting down. To ease themselves they go indoors . . . on the theory that what is unseemly but necessary should be done in private."[9] As for bathing, poorer folk relied on bowls or pitchers of water filled at the river and lugged inside, perhaps to a bedroom. They washed their hands, face, or other body parts (today called a sponge bath) and dumped the dirty water outside.

Poorer homes not only lacked bathing facilities but also had far fewer rooms. The average lower-class townhouse had three or four small rooms. The main room had a dais (a raised, flat platform) running around part of its perimeter for people to sit on or use to prepare food or stack belongings. Some bedrooms had daises, too, on which family members placed reed mats, creating primitive beds. Otherwise, the sparse furnishings consisted of a few stools and storage chests. As in richer homes, the roofs were also used for storage (as well as for sleeping on hot summer nights).

Making the small rooms even more cramped was the common custom of stabling one's donkey, goats, and other animals inside the house. Herodotus pointedly observed about the Egyptians, "They live with their animals, unlike [people in]the rest of the world, who live apart from them."[10] Fortunately for the family, when the animals relieved themselves indoors, the mess was fairly easy to clean up since the floors were generally made of dirt, sometimes covered with reed mats.

The other structural aspects of poorer homes were equally basic and inexpensive. Most such structures were made from mud bricks, one of the mainstays of construction in the ancient Near East (or Middle East). People made these bricks by adding water and chopped straw to clay; kneading the mixture (usually by walking on it); pressing it into oblong, flat bricks; and finally laying the bricks out in the sun to dry. One advantage of mud bricks was that they were poor conductors of heat, which kept the interiors of houses cooler on hot days. The main disadvantage of the clay bricks was that they decomposed rather rapidly. As a result, homeowners had to do frequent repairs, and over time such houses crumbled back into Egypt's soil, leaving few traces (often to the frustration of modern archaeologists!).

The ceilings and roofs of such houses were made from materials that were even more perishable and impermanent. Surviving models of some Middle Kingdom houses show that most ceilings were covered with clusters of wooden beams laid next to one another. Over the beams workmen placed a layer of palm fronds, bundles of reeds, or clay bricks and then covered everything with a layer of fine mud. Most such roofs featured stairs along one side so that people could walk up onto the roof and use it for storage or simply for relaxing.

The homes of the rural poor, also constructed of mud bricks, branches, reeds, and other perishable materials, were often (though certainly not always) even smaller and more primitive than those of the urban poor. Many rural houses, which stood near the farmers' fields or in small villages, had only one to three rooms. In such abodes, life for a family of four, five, or six people plus their animals must have been cramped and uncomfortable. There was a pronounced lack of privacy (though this may not have bothered the Egyptians as much it would people today). And with people living in such close proximity to animals and their waste materials, sanitary conditions were poor to say the least.

Family Size

Whether they lived in small, squalid houses or large, comfortable ones, all Egyptians took pride in their families. The average size of the family in ancient Egypt is somewhat difficult to discern, partly because the surviving evidence is sketchy and also because most families changed in size over time. A couple might have more and more children. But some of these children might die, and others would inevitably leave home to start their own households and families. Fragments of a community register of

Decorative Home Gardens

Gardens were often important aspects of Egyptian homes. Indeed, the Egyptians prized flowers and plants of all kinds, including those that decorated their houses. Not surprisingly, the most elaborate gardens were those of the wealthy. A typical example had tall walls around the perimeter to provide privacy and featured subdivisions that included different kinds of trees, bushes, and flowers. Most gardens followed neat, orderly arrangements, with trees, bushes, and other plants lined up in straight rows. It was also common to have a pond with fish and floating water plants. Even poorer townhouses were, when the owners could manage it, decorated with shrubs and flowers, usually planted in clay pots similar to those in use today.

This tomb painting dating from the thirteenth century B.C. shows a man watering plants in a garden.

families have been recovered from the workers' village at Deir el-Medina. And of thirty couples mentioned, one had four children, five had three, six had two, seven had one, and four had none. (The rest of these households were occupied by unmarried males.)

These figures suggest a ratio of children per household fairly similar to that in modern developed countries like the United States. However, this picture could well be deceiving. First, there is no way to know if the size and makeup of the families at Deir el-Medina were typical for Egypt as a whole. Also, although only parents and children are mentioned in the surviving register, some extended family members—grandparents, cousins, in-laws, and so forth—may have been present, too. One must not assume that, because most of the houses at Deir el-Medina were relatively small, there was no room for such large families. As Gay Robins points out, such assumptions

> may be due to modern Western ideas of privacy. Much of life [in ancient Egypt] could have been lived outdoors in the street or on the roof, and at night the floor would have become sleeping space. Any expectation of privacy might simply not have existed.[11]

Whatever the actual size of the average family in Egypt, the ideal may have been for the father, who was the head of the household, and the mother, who ran the house, to have as many children as possible. At least this seems to have been the case in the era directly following the New Kingdom. A series of maxims known as the *Instruction of Any*, dating from the eleventh or tenth century B.C. advises: "It is proper [for parents] to make [children]. Happy [is] the man whose [children] are many. He is saluted [by his friends] on account of his progeny [offspring]."[12] At first glance this philosophy does not appear to be reflected in the census figures from Deir el-Medina. But the fact that many families in the village ended up with four or fewer children may not reflect the actual number of children born there. Indeed, because of poor sanitation, ignorance of the causes of disease, and other factors, infant mortality was high in ancient times. Rates of children dying in infancy or childhood were possibly as high as 20 to 50 percent at any given time and place in ancient Egypt.

Childrens' Lives and Obligations

Children who did survive were generally breastfed by their mothers. No social taboos existed about doing so in public, as shown in a number of surviving relief sculptures showing nursing mothers, including a few royal queens and princesses nursing. However, some royal women, along with poorer women who could not produce enough milk to nurse, turned to wet nurses. The wet nurses generally came from lower-class families and were usually paid for their services. If a family could afford it, they had the wet nurse move into the house. Sometimes these women developed extremely close relationships with the children they nursed, and in the royal household this might even translate into a marked raise in status. For example, the pharaoh Thutmose III (reigned 1479–1425 B.C.) chose as his chief wife the daughter of his former wet nurse.

When they were old enough, Egyptian children played with toys, a great many of them similar to those modern children play with. Among these were dolls, puppets, tops, and miniature weapons (swords, axes, bows and arrows, and chariots). Balls were also widely popular, and depictions of a wide variety of ball games have survived in paintings and sculptures. In one wall painting, two girls throw a small ball back and forth while their friends clap their hands, evidently to keep time. Another painting shows a ball game in which teams of two children each were involved. One teammate carried the other piggyback while his or her partner tossed a ball to the top partner of another team.

Children's lives did not consist only of play, however. For example, the sons of farmers and tradesmen often began learning their father's work before they were ten. Similarly, young women helped their mothers cook, clean, and make clothes when they were as young as seven or eight (and perhaps even younger in some families).

Whatever the nature of their fathers' professions, some evidence suggests that all boys went through a rite of passage from youth to young manhood at about age fourteen. The ceremony, called *sebi*, was attended by family, friends, and community members and typically included

Children's dolls often had wooden torsos like these. Hair and other details were added to the torsos.

circumcision. A stela (marker stone) from the First Intermediate Period (ca. 2181–2155 B.C.) shows 120 boys undergoing circumcision at the same time. The rite was performed by a priest with a ceremonial hooked knife made of flint, and because no anesthetic was used, it must have been painful.

Both before and after their manhood ceremony, boys (as well as girls) were expected to obey their elders, especially their parents. In his list of adages, the Old

Kingdom administrator Ptahhotep emphasized the need for discipline and punishment for unruly offspring: "If he [the child] strays, neglects your counsel, [and] disobeys all that is said [by the parents], his mouth spouting evil speech, punish him for all his talk!" In contrast, said Ptahhotep, "If he is straight, takes after you, [and] takes good care of your possessions, do for him all that is good."[13] A good son (or grandson or nephew if the son was dead) was also expected to help care for his parents in their old age. In addition, a son (or other male relative) made the funeral arrangements for the parents.

Servants and Slaves

Whatever work the children did around the house was secondary to that performed by servants and slaves (in those households that had servants and slaves). Wealthy households, including the royal palace, of course, had many menial workers; in fact, these larger homes could not have operated efficiently without the aid of a considerable amount of cheap labor. Middle-class and poorer households had servants and slaves, too, though fewer than rich ones. Still, even someone of limited means could own a surprisingly large number of slaves

Servants pluck geese in this wall painting from a New Kingdom tomb. It is often difficult to distinguish servants from slaves in such paintings.

if that person devoted a large enough portion of his or her income to purchasing them. Consider a lower-class worker named Ken who lived at Deir el-Medina. Evidence shows that he owned twelve slaves.

At least scholars assume that Ken's helpers were slaves he owned and not servants to whom he paid salaries. (It is presumed that on his own meager salary he could not have afforded to employ paid servants.) The fact is that it is often difficult for modern observers to differentiate between free servants and unfree slaves in ancient Egypt. Indeed, arriving at a clear-cut definition for a slave in that society is equally difficult. This is because ancient Egyptian slavery was not like the more familiar kind practiced in ancient Rome and pre–Civil War America. In the latter two societies, slaves were people who lacked all civil and legal rights; they could not own property or marry free persons and could be abused and, at times, even killed, more or less with impunity.

In contrast, though Egyptian slaves could be bought, sold, or rented out, they possessed certain basic rights. First, they could earn money and own property, including land, and dispose of either as they wished. They could also marry whomever they wanted, including free persons. Thus, true slaves—those lacking all rights—did not exist in ancient Egypt.

This does not mean that all Egyptian slaves were well off. A majority were war prisoners or convicts, and the rest were poor peasants or the children born of slaves. They were expected to do as their masters ordered, no matter how menial or embarrassing, and their movements were severely restricted. Most slaves worked long hours on large agricultural estates run by nobles and temple priests. Others labored in the mines that produced metal ores or precious and semiprecious stones. (Common modern depictions of large groups of slaves toiling to erect Egypt's pyramids and other large-scale monuments are erroneous; the vast majority of these workers were free agricultural peasants enlisted for such work when they were not planting or harvesting their crops.)

Regarding the treatment of slaves, the surviving evidence is slim. But it is fairly well established that the mine workers had the worst and shortest lives, especially in the Late and Ptolemaic periods, when non-Egyptian rulers controlled Egypt. Household slaves appear to have been much better treated and to have had a better chance of gaining their freedom. Exactly how they went about gaining their freedom is unknown, as are most other aspects of their lives, since writers, who belonged to the middle and upper classes, rarely mentioned them. What is certain is that servants or slaves of some kind played crucial roles in maintaining many Egyptian homes and families. And families were the pillars on which society rested.

Chapter Two

WOMEN VS. MEN: LOVE, MARRIAGE, AND DIVORCE

Like other ancient lands, Egypt had a largely male-dominated society. A handful of female pharaohs ruled the country during its long history, and the wives and daughters of kings at times indirectly influenced state policy. But these were rare exceptions. In general, women had no political rights and men ran the government, religious temples, courts, and other important institutions. Most women got married, kept house (including cooking, baking, and making clothes), and raised children.

Nevertheless, even considering these traditional roles and restrictions on their lives and authority, Egyptian women enjoyed a surprising degree of personal freedom and legal and economic rights. Indeed, throughout the Old, Middle, and New kingdoms, they had more legal rights than women in most other ancient lands and even in some modern ones. An Egyptian woman could own, inherit, and bequeath land and other property, for example. She could retain her property during and after a marriage as well. Egyptian women could also enter into legally binding contracts. Examples of such contracts—made with husbands, wet nurses, merchants, gardeners, and others—have survived. A woman could sue someone in court, something unheard-of in ancient Greece, where people fancied themselves more enlightened than the Egyptians.

In addition, Egyptian women had complete freedom of movement (another privilege many Greek women lacked), which allowed large numbers of them to work outside the home. Some labored in workshops where fabric was spun and clothes were made; others were assistants to bakers or millers; others worked in fields sowing and harvesting crops; and still others made a living as singers, dancers, musicians, or hairdressers. Moreover, some modern scholars think that those Egyptian women who did work received pay equal to that of men in the same jobs. (To date,

These colorful wall paintings show typical female activities, including spinning and weaving (top two panels) and music making.

the United States has yet to attain that level of economic parity.)

With so many legal and economic rights, women were potentially a force to reckon with in Egyptian society. These rights meant that women did not need to be subservient to men in order to survive economically. The following advice that the Old Kingdom sage Ptahhotep gave to men entering marriage shows that men did not always have the upper hand in a typical household:

> When you prosper and found your house, and love your wife with ardor, fill her belly, clothe her back. Ointment soothes her body [so make sure she has plenty of it]. Gladden her heart as

Ode to a Girl with Dancing Eyes

This eloquent love song from the late New Kingdom, one of several such songs that have survived, is translated in John L. Foster's collection of Egyptian literature.

My love is one and only, without peer, lovely above all Egypt's lovely girls. On the horizon of my seeing, [I] see her, rising, glistening goddess of the sunrise star [the planet Venus] bright in the forehead of a lucky year. So there she stands, epitome of shining, shedding light, her eyebrows gleaming darkly, marking eyes which dance and wander. Sweet are those lips, which chatter (but never a word too much), and the line of the long neck, lovely, dropping . . . to young breasts firm in the bouncing light which shimmers that blue-shadowed sidefall of hair. And slim are those arms, over-toned with gold [jewelry], those fingers which touch like a brush of lotus [a delicate water plant].

long as you live, [for]she is a fertile field for her lord. Do not contend with her in court [where she can cause trouble for you], [but]keep her from [such exercise of]power, restrain her. . . . [In these ways]will you make her stay in your house [and have a smooth and pleasant existence].[14]

Love and Its Pursuit

One of Ptahhotep's phrases stands out to the modern eye, namely "love your wife with ardor." In most ancient societies the vast majority of marriages were arranged by relatives, usually fathers and/or male clan leaders. Love rarely played a part (at least in the beginning, as some husbands and wives grew to love each other over time). In Egypt, too, it appears that many marriages were arranged. But evidence suggests that relationships built on romantic love were more common there than in most other ancient lands.

Part of the evidence for the existence of true love in ancient Egypt is found in paintings, sculptures, and jewelry produced for members of the upper classes. Particularly memorable are a group of scarabs (jewelry pieces shaped like beetles) commissioned by the pharaoh Amenhotep III (reigned ca. 1390–1352 B.C.) to commemorate his marriage to his queen, Tiy (or Teye). The inscription makes a point of calling Tiy his principal wife (he had a harem that included several wives), a nicety that was unnecessary and therefore likely motivated out of love. Amenhotep also had a statue of Tiy equal in size to one of himself set up in his mortuary temple in Thebes. (Normally, statues and painted images of wives, children, and others were a good deal smaller than those of the pharaohs.) In addition, Tiy was a commoner. And as noted scholar Eugen Strouhal points out, "Since she was not of royal blood, it must indeed have been a love match."[15]

The relationship between Amenhotep's

successor, Akhenaten (ca. 1352–1336 B.C.) and his own chief wife, Nefertiti, also seems to have been based on deep love and affection. Numerous paintings from Akhenaten's reign depict the royal couple enjoying life together. Some images even go so far as to show them embracing and kissing in public, which was unusual for Egyptian royal art.

Royals and other rich and famous people were not the only ones who married for love. This fact is revealed by statements made in a number of letters and tomb writings that have survived. A large number of love songs have also survived, mostly, but by no means exclusively, from the New Kingdom. The following example from the latter part of that era consists of a young woman's longings for her husband or lover, who is far away (perhaps on a military campaign or ocean voyage):

I love you through the daytimes, in the dark, through all the long divisions of the night, those hours [that] I, spendthrift, waste away alone, and lie, and turn, awake till whitened dawn. And with the shape of you I people [my] nights, and thoughts of hot desire grow and live within me. What magic was it in that voice of yours to bring such singing vigor to my flesh, to limbs which now lie listless on my bed without you?[16]

The desire by both women and men to find love is also attested by the widespread use of magic spells designed for that purpose. The Egyptians considered magic to be a potent supplement to religious faith because they envisioned spells working through the innate powers of the gods. To get a spell to work, therefore, one invoked the name of an appropriate god. A man wrote the following love spell on an ostrakon during the late New Kingdom:

Akhenaten and Nefertiti demonstrate their affection for each other by holding hands in this limestone carving.

Hear me, O Ra [the Sun god]...father of the gods.... O hear, all you gods of heaven and Earth! Grant that this girl, true child of her mother, pursue me with undying passion, [that she will] follow close on my heels like a cow seeking pasture, like a nursemaid minding her charge, like a guardian after his herd! For if you will not cause her to love me, I must surely abandon the day, consumed to dust in the fire of my burning.[17]

Choosing a Mate

Usually the end product of any mutual feelings of love between men and women was marriage. Of course, love was not the only factor driving this institution so common in all cultures. Equally or perhaps more important was perpetuating the family and its name by producing children, preferably at least one of them a male since men headed most households. In his list of wise sayings, the sage Any said, "Take a wife while you're young, that she may make a son for you."[18]

It is difficult to discern what age Any had in mind when he urged men to marry "young." It has already been established that young men in Egypt took part in manhood rites when they were roughly fourteen. Presumably they were free to marry at that point. But other snippets of evidence point to an average marriage age for males of between fifteen and twenty. The evidence also suggests that girls tended to get married when they were somewhat younger, most often shortly after they

reached puberty—between the ages of twelve and fourteen. (Cases mentioned in the ancient sources in which girls married when they were eight, nine, or ten appear to have been exceptional.)

As for whom one chose for a mate, there were few social and other barriers. Most people married within their socioeconomic class (that is, poor people tended to marry other poor people, and rich people usually married other rich people). But this was mainly because a person was more likely to meet and get to know someone from his or her own class. There do not seem to have been any legal sanctions against marrying someone of a different class. Race and foreign extraction also presented no barriers to marriage. Native Egyptians (who were olive-skinned, like many of today's Arabs and Israelis) sometimes married black Nubians (from Nubia, the region lying directly south of Egypt) or people from foreign lands.

Many Egyptians also married within the family. Unions between cousins were fairly common, as were those between uncles and nieces and stepbrothers and stepsisters. Contrary to popular belief, marriages between actual brothers and sisters were quite rare among nonroyals. A study by the late Czech Egyptologist Jaroslav Cerny of 490 average Egyptian marriages spanning the Middle Kingdom found only two cases involving brothers and sisters. In contrast, the custom was fairly common in royal families because kings and queens were supposed to emulate the gods. Specifically, it was thought that Osiris, lord of the Underworld, married his sister, the fertil-

Political necessity could dictate a pharaoh's choice of wife. To connect himself to the royal family, Horemheb (right) married Nefertiti's sister.

ity goddess Isis, producing a son—the god Horus—and that divine union provided a model for human royalty.

Another marriage custom practiced mainly by royalty, along with those few wealthy men who could afford it, was taking multiple wives. Most pharaohs had harems attended by their own staffs of cooks, servants, and security guards. There was no law against commoners having more than one wife, but it was clearly an expensive proposition. And monogamy

seems to have been the rule for the vast majority of Egyptians, as noted by Herodotus following his stay in the country in the Late Period. Confirmation of his observation comes from archaeological studies of the layout of the houses in the workers' village at Deir el-Medina, where the homes were not designed to accommodate families containing multiple wives. Also, the surviving portions of the village register do not list any multiple marriages. Thus, such marriages were probably

Complaint to a Dead Wife

One interesting aspect of relationships between Egyptian husbands and wives was that when one partner died the survivor often wrote letters to the deceased. This was based on the belief that a person's spirit lived on in the afterlife and could affect the lives of the living. The letter excerpted here (from Mayers and Prideaux's Never to Die*) was written by a man who blamed his present misfortunes on his dead wife.*

What wicked thing have I done to you that I should come to this evil pass [occurrence]? What have I done to you? But what *you* have done is to have laid hands on me, although I have done nothing wicked to you. From the time I lived with you as your husband, down to today, what have I done to you that I need hide? . . . You do not recognize the good which I have done to you, so I write to let you know what you are doing [by making my life miserable]. When you were sick . . . I caused a master physician to be fetched, and he gave you treatment and did everything which you did command. . . . But behold, you do not know good from bad. Therefore, judgment shall be made between you and me.

exceedingly rare among Egyptians of average means. (The exception was during the Ptolemaic Period, when, according to Diodorus Siculus, an upsurge in multiple marriages occurred in the middle and lower classes.)

Getting Married

Throughout most of Egypt's ancient history weddings were better described as celebrations rather than ceremonies because they had social, rather than legal or religious, significance. Relatives and friends got together for a big party that included feasting, singing, dancing, and storytelling. But there were no religious or civil sanctions or rituals. All available evidence indicates that once the bride moved into the groom's house, the marriage was in force. Eventually, beginning in the Third Intermediate Period (ca. 1069–747 B.C.), some written marriage contracts appeared. But these seem to have been mainly concerned with the property rights of the wife and children rather than with sanctifying marriage itself.

Another relatively late development was the formal dowry (money or goods the bride's family supplied for her maintenance in the marriage). Egyptian women long enjoyed the right to share in and control the assets of their marriages along with their husbands. So dowries seem to have been optional and fairly rare before the onset of Greek cultural influences in the Late and Ptolemaic periods. (Greek women had few economic rights, so dowries were important components of their marriages.)

As for how husbands and wives interacted and treated each other after setting up their households, the evidence is scarce. But scattered remarks in ancient writings suggest that many men allowed their wives considerable latitude in running the house and in making family decisions. Although society was male dominated, wiser Egyptian men learned that it was unproductive for men to be bossy on a regular basis. Advice for achieving harmony between husband and wife is included in the *Instruction of Any*:

> Do not control your wife in her house when you know she is efficient. Don't say to her, "Where is it? Get it!" when she has put it in the right place. Let your eye observe in silence. Then you [will]recognize her skill [for which she will be thankful]. . . . There are many [men]who don't know this [wisdom]. If a man desists from strife at home, he will not encounter its beginning. Every man who founds a household should hold back the hasty heart [i.e., think and reason before acting in haste in marital matters].[19]

Reasons for Divorce

But no matter how much husbands and wives might strive for harmony and happiness, some Egyptian marriages ended in divorce. The reasons for divorce in Egypt were similar to many today. They included, for instance, the inability of a wife to bear children (perhaps in some cases her failure to produce male children); involve-

ment of one partner in a serious crime; or the desire of either husband or wife to marry someone else.

Probably the most common reason for divorce, however, was adultery. Almost always it was the wife who was accused of infidelity because society generally allowed men greater latitude in having extramarital

A stela from the Middle Kingdom shows a man named Hornakhte and his wife.

affairs. Such an accusation was a very serious matter, as the evidence is overwhelming that society heavily frowned on adultery. A passage in the *Instruction of Any* warns:

> Beware of a woman who is a stranger, one not known in her town. Don't stare at her when she goes by. Do not know her carnally [sexually]. A deep water whose course is unknown, such is a woman [who is] away from her husband. "I am pretty," she tells you daily, when she has no witnesses [i.e., when you and she are alone]. She is ready to ensnare you, a great deadly crime when it is heard.[20]

A more graphic indication of the disdain most people had for adultery takes the form of fragments of a letter written by a resident of Deir el-Medina during the New Kingdom. It seems that a married man named Nesamenemipet was having a not-so-secret affair with a woman in the village. Per custom, people did not hold him responsible but instead blamed the "other woman" for entrapping him. The indignant neighbors finally decided to act, and a crowd formed with every intention of beating her. At the last moment, however, an unnamed local official stepped in. He offered to protect the woman from the crowd if Nesamenemipet agreed to get a proper divorce from his wife before continuing his relationship with the other woman. One can conclude from this incident that pressures from one's neighbors and peers discouraged certain kinds of bad behavior in the community, including adultery. It remains unknown whether these pressures existed throughout Egypt, but it seems likely.

Some men were willing to endure the inconvenience of divorce to advance their professional and social positions. Evidence suggests that a number of young men who worked as government administrators used divorce and remarriage to better their chances of climbing the bureaucratic ladder. For example, a man might leave his existing wife and marry the boss's daughter, ensuring a promotion. In a letter to his dead wife, to whom he remained ever loyal, one administrator boasted that he had *not* used this apparently common means of career advancement:

> When I was a young man, I was with you when I was carrying out all sorts of [government] offices. I was with you and I did not divorce you [as so many others in my profession might have]. I did not cause your heart to grieve. . . . [While] I was carrying out all sorts of important offices for [the] Pharaoh . . . without divorcing you . . . [I said,] "She has always been with me." So said I![21]

The Divorce Process

Whatever the reasons for the breakup, evidently the first thing that happened in a divorce was the departure of one party from the house. Because most houses were owned by men, this usually meant that the husband asked or ordered the wife to leave. This might happen more than once to the same couple if they quarreled frequently, as shown in a surviving financial record. A workman named Khnum-mose recorded how he became involved in the marriage squabbles of a friend named Ruty:

His wife spent forty days dwelling with me in my house [because she had nowhere else to go?], and I provided for her, giving her one sack of emmer [wheat]and ten loaves [of bread]. And he threw her out again, and she spent twenty days in the house of [our mutual friend?] Menna, while I supplied 3 sacks of emmer, 1 [garment], [and]1 measure of fruit.[22]

In those rarer cases in which a woman owned the house that she and a man lived in, a breakup meant that he had to leave. In a surviving document, a man lists all of the goods he brought into the house, including two containers of sesame seed oil, two pairs of sandals, a sleeping mat, a headrest, two bowls, some jewelry, and many food items. He then states, "And she threw me out, although she had not made [for] me [even] a garment [to cover]my behind. I went again with all my property in order to live with her. Look, she acted exactly the same way [by throwing me out]again!"[23] This probably atypical situation aside, it is unclear whether women often initiated divorce during the Old, Middle, and New kingdoms. The consensus of scholarly opinion is that they did not and that female-initiated divorce did not begin in earnest until the late sixth century B.C., when Egypt was controlled by the Persian Empire.

A Husband Threatens Divorce

This letter, written by a female resident of the village of Deir el-Medina to her sister (quoted in A.G. McDowell's Village Life in Ancient Egypt*), complains of an overly demanding husband who has threatened to evict his wife if her family does not give him food and other supplies.*

I will send this grain to you and you should have it ground for me and add emmer [wheat] to it and make it into bread for me, because I am quarreling with [my husband] Mery-Ma'at. "I'll throw you out!" so he says, and he quarrels with my mother, enquiring after [trying to get her to give him] grain for [his] bread. "Now, your mother does not do anything for you!" so he says to me, saying [also] "now, you have siblings, but they do not look after you!" So he says, arguing with me daily.

The departure of one party from the house was only the first step in the divorce process. Although nothing formal and legal was required for a marriage, custom dictated a bit more formality for a divorce. According to James Romano:

Tradition required that the dissolution of a marriage be accompanied by a divorce agreement which contained a clause that the rejected partner was henceforth free to remarry. If a man left his wife for any reason but adultery, he was obliged to pay her a lump sum equivalent to one-third of his property plus a "divorce penalty." A house that belonged to the woman before the marriage remained hers, and the man was obliged to vacate; otherwise, she had to relinquish [give up] all claims to the home.[24]

Thus, the breakup of a marriage almost always caused some kind of economic hardship for one or both parties (in addition to the expected emotional upsets). Perhaps this is one reason that divorce was fairly uncommon in ancient Egypt. The possibility that a high proportion of marriages were love matches should not be dismissed as another reason for the low divorce rate. One thing is certain: Whatever social traditions and family dynamics affected marriage in ancient Egypt, the results were usually positive, as most people who mated did so for life.

Chapter Three

PERSONAL CARE: DRESS, GROOMING, AND HEALTH

The ancient Egyptians, both rich and poor, were extremely concerned with their personal appearance. This fact is repeatedly illustrated in their paintings, sculptures, and other artistic images, which almost always show clean, well-groomed men, women, and children. Clothing styles were often simple (with the exception of some wealthy people in certain eras). Indeed, clothes were often relatively skimpy by today's standards, not surprising given Egypt's hot climate. But whether their outfits were simple or elaborate, whenever possible people kept their clothes well laundered. "They wear linen clothes which they make a special point of continually washing,"[25] Herodotus observed. They also adorned themselves with jewelry and freely used skin lotions, cosmetics, and even wigs to enhance their looks.

Going hand and hand with this concern for physical appearance was the hope and desire for good health and general well-being. Like people in all societies through-out history, the Egyptians suffered from a wide range of illnesses, injuries, and diseases. In fact, because of their ignorance of the existence of germs and their lack of proper sanitation (by modern standards), they were more susceptible to a number of ailments that only rarely cause problems today. The Egyptians attempted to meet the health-care challenge by developing a rich medical tradition. Some of their cures were effective and others were not. Yet even the ineffective ones (notably those that employed magic spells) may sometimes have been helpful. The patients sincerely believed these cures were viable and therefore benefited at least psychologically.

Basic Clothing

Sick or not, people certainly felt better about themselves if they were well dressed. Most clothes worn in ancient Egypt were made from linen, which derived from fibers of flax, a plant widely grown in the country. Clothing styles in the Old and Middle kingdoms tended to be rather simple. Men, particularly in the upper classes, wore a kilt made by wrapping a rectangular piece of cloth around the waist. The garment usually hung to the knees. Farmers and laborers generally made do with a basic linen loincloth or apron, although some owned kilts to wear on special occasions. (It is sometimes difficult to know who wore what and when because most of what is known about Egyptian clothing comes from artistic renderings. And these often used artistic conventions that depicted people more stylistically than realistically. Thus, the traditional and most accepted way of showing a worker in art

was in a loincloth or an apron, even if he sometimes wore other garments.)

In the same periods most women, both rich and poor, wore a linen sheath dress made by forming a large piece of cloth into a tube and sewing up one side. Again, artistic renderings can be deceiving. Most paintings depict these dresses as clinging to the body very tightly, as if they were made of a spandexlike material. "In most cases the dress hugs the body with no slack," Gay Robins points out,

so that the wearer appears to be hobbled. Most formal female figures [shown in art] have their feet almost together [another common convention]. When a figure needs to be

An early modern drawing shows a mix of Egyptian fashions from the New Kingdom and later periods.

Looms for Making Cloth

The Egyptians used primitive but effective looms to weave thread into cloth. Up until the end of the Middle Kingdom, the typical loom consisted of four narrow horizontal poles held up by pegs set in the ground, forming a square-shaped frame. The weavers, who most often worked in groups of two or more, attached the spindle that held the thread to a stick standing vertically next to the loom. Pulling thread from the spindle, one weaver connected the end of the thread to a stick, called the shuttle, after which a second worker moved the shuttle under and over several threads running at right angles to it. At the appropriate moment the second weaver tossed the shuttle to the first, or a third, weaver sitting on the other side of the loom. And this process was repeated until the piece of cloth was finished. A slightly more advanced loom appeared shortly before the beginning of the New Kingdom. Although it, too, had a square-shaped wooden frame, it stood in a vertical position and the weavers interwove the threads from the bottom up.

This pottery model shows a group of women using a horizontal loom to weave cloth.

shown in movement, the dress is extended just enough to allow this, as though it were elastic. . . . It is clear that the image is an artistic one and not one that could have existed in reality.[26]

Indeed, the few surviving dresses from that era are fairly loose and even baggy rather than completely formfitting. The convention of showing them as tight fitting, which revealed the shape of the breasts and lines of tummy and hips, may have been designed to emphasize female sexuality.

In the New Kingdom, the clothes of the upper classes became more elaborate. Men still wore the kilt, but more as an undergarment. Over it they donned a tunic, usually made from very thin, almost transparent

A painting from the New Kingdom shows men wearing traditional loincloths and kilts and a woman in a tight-fitting dress.

linen, that stretched to midcalf or sometimes lower. Linen shirts with short sleeves were also common. Women's dresses got longer and often featured elegant pleats and fringes. Poorer men and women continued to wear simple dresses, kilts, and loincloths. Most clothes in this and prior eras were white, although some were dyed yellow, red, or blue. Also, wool cloaks were sometimes worn on cold nights. (Wool always remained less popular than linen in Egypt, partly because religious taboos forbade placing certain animal products, including wool, in tombs.)

In the Ptolemaic Period, when Greeks ruled Egypt and many Greeks immigrat-ed there, Greek fashions became influen-tial, especially in upper-class circles. This included the use of the himation, a cloak-like garment worn over a tunic or dress. Eventually, some members of the lower classes adopted Greek-style clothes, although the poorest Egyptians still tend-ed to dress as their ancestors had.

Shoes and Hair

Like so many other aspects of Egyptian clothing, footwear tended to be fairly sim-ple. It appears that many Egyptians went barefoot most of the time. This is not surprising, as even today millions of people living in northern Africa go barefoot their whole lives. For formal occasions or when the terrain or custom dictated some form of footwear, sandals were the main kind of shoe. Average Egyptians wore sandals made from interwoven strands of tough grasses. Sandals worn by members of the upper classes were more often made of leather. Whatever sandals were made of, most were held in place by three thongs, one of which passed between the first and second toes, the others from the back of the ankle to the top of the foot.

There were specific rules of etiquette surrounding the use of sandals. It was viewed as a common courtesy, for instance, for a person wearing sandals to take them off when he or she encountered a person of authority or higher social class. It was also customary to remove one's sandals or other footwear when worshipping a god.

One would also have removed one's hat in the presence of royalty or a god if hats were common in Egypt, as they were in Greece. However, very few Egyptians wore hats or other kinds of headgear (until Ptolemaic times, when the Greeks introduced them). A number of modern films have portrayed Egyptians of all classes wearing the *nemes*, a cloth headdress that folded so that the sides flared outward. But this is inaccurate, as the *nemes* was more or less restricted to the Egyptian royal family. The only societal group whose members covered their heads on a regular basis were

These sandals were once worn by Nefertari, queen of the pharaoh Ramesses II. They were found in her tomb in the Valley of the Queens.

grain harvesters; they tied cloth kerchiefs around their heads to prevent loose wheat chaff from getting entangled in their hair.

In the absence of hats, Egyptians avoided sunburning their heads by using wigs, which became items of fashion as well as protection. Both men and women regularly wore wigs when in public throughout the Old, Middle, and New kingdoms. The recent discovery by Polish archaeologists of an eleventh-century B.C. wig-making shop shows that a net of interwoven fabric threads served as the foundation of a wig. Human hair (or less often plant fibers) were attached to the net and then combed out. Shaping was accomplished by cutting with sharp knives and applying wax to create permanent waves in the places desired.

As for facial hair, in the Predynastic Period (ca. 5500–3100 B.C.) it appears that Egyptian men wore full beards. But some of the early pharaohs began shaving their faces, which quickly set a trend that the masses followed. From then on, with the exception of an occasional mustache or thin tuft of hair under the chin, men were clean shaven. (The exception was during periods of mourning for the dead, when it was permissible, and indeed common, for men to go unshaven.) At first men shaved with sharpened stone blades set in wooden handles; later, copper and then bronze blades replaced the stone ones.

This painted limestone bust of Nofret, chief queen of King Senusret II, shows her wearing a wig. Both men and women wore wigs.

Female guests at a banquet prepare to wash and apply perfume. It was customary to wash the hands and face both before and after eating.

Personal Grooming

Shaving was only one aspect of the widespread practice of personal grooming in ancient Egypt. Abundant evidence demonstrates that the Egyptians were very concerned about cleanliness and were almost ritualistic about washing and bathing. Nearly everyone, rich or poor, had at least a sponge bath once a day. And those who worked in jobs in which sweating and getting dirty were routine washed their bodies more than once a day. It was also common for people to wash their hands and face both before and after meals. (This had the beneficial effect of reducing the spread of germ-borne diseases, though this was not the intended goal of the behavior since the Egyptians did not know of the existence of germs.)

Another daily cleanliness ritual was rinsing the mouth with natron (mineral salts) dissolved in water. People called it *sen shem shem*, meaning "cleansing of mouth and teeth."

It was also common to supplement daily bathing routines with skin care. The sun's hot rays and the effects of wind and sand are pronounced in Egypt and can be very damaging to the skin. In response, many (if not most) Egyptians rubbed themselves with lotions at least once a day. Lotions were made from animal fat (from hippopotamuses, crocodiles, cats, and sheep) and various combinations of vegetable oils, such as castor bean oil. People kept their rubbing oil in small lidded jars made of pottery, wood, glass, or ivory. The wealthy went further and applied supposed antiwrinkle creams, one composed of a mixture of vegetable oil, frankincense, fermented fruit juice, and grass.

The use of deodorants to mask body odors was also widespread. Poor people rubbed themselves with ground roots, such as carob, while the well-to-do could afford fragrant perfumes. In fact, Egypt became famous for its production of perfumes, which were exported throughout the Mediterranean world, especially during the country's Greek and Roman periods. The finer perfumes were made by mixing spices such as myrrh, frankincense, or desert date with animal fat or vegetable oil.

In addition, as numerous surviving paintings attest, Egyptian women (and quite a few men, too) made liberal use of cosmetics. The earliest known eye makeup was green, made by crushing a copper

An exhibit at the Louvre in Paris displays containers used for eye shadow and other cosmetics. Many Egyptian women used makeup liberally.

oxide called malachite into a powder. This remained widely popular from the late Predynastic Period to Roman times. But by the early New Kingdom a black eyeliner called *khol* had become even more popular. *Khol* powder was made by grinding up various lead compounds. A person applied such makeup by wetting a finger or small stick with water or oil, dipping it into the powder, and then rubbing it into the skin. To add color to the cheeks, people used a rouge made from a powdered mixture of red ocher (an iron oxide); adding fat or tree resins to this powder produced a widely used lipstick.

Common Health Hazards

Clothing, wigs, skin lotions, perfumes, and makeup were all external items designed, at least in part, to enhance a person's appearance and personal feelings of well-being. But as with people in all times and places, often these feelings proved secondary to one's actual physical well-being. Even in modern industrialized nations like the United States, tens of million of people get sick each year, necessitating the existence of an immense health care industry. At least knowledge of germs and modern advances in sanitation and scientific medicine have greatly reduced the incidence of contracting and dying from a number of illnesses.

In ancient lands like Egypt, by contrast, ignorance of the causes of disease, coupled with poor sanitation and other factors, caused widespread misery on a regular basis. Overcrowding and inadequate ventilation in houses were common, for example. Many people regularly breathed in the airborne sweat and exhalations of relatives and family animals, promoting lung infections and the spread of infectious diseases such as tuberculosis.

Insects, especially flies and mosquitoes, also spread disease on a scale seen today only in the most impoverished third world countries. "Flitting from rubbish to food," Eugen Strouhal writes, flies

disseminated [spread] intestinal infections, notably amoebic dysentery [and] typhoid and paratyphoid fevers. Flies were so numerous that people ceased to notice them and children did not even brush them off their skin or even from their eyes, whence the prevalence of trachoma, leading to a serious [impairment of the eyes] and even blindness. . . . Another scourge, mainly in the [Nile] Delta and in areas that were marshy, were the mosquitoes which became particularly abundant in October and November as the [yearly Nile] floods receded. . . . The *Anopheles* mosquito carried the [germs] responsible for malaria.[27]

People tried to combat such pests as best as they could. "South of the marshes," Herodotus reported in his *Histories*,

they sleep at night on raised structures, which is a great benefit to them because the [insects] are prevented by the wind from flying high. In the marsh country itself . . . everyone instead provides himself with a net,

Egyptian homes, like that shown in this limestone model, were often infested with pests.

also sometimes carried fleas infected with bubonic plague. Greek and Roman writers confirmed a number of outbreaks of this fatal disease in Egypt.

Compounding the ill effects of overcrowding and pests were a host of traditional unsanitary practices. Though the Egyptians were meticulous about keeping their bodies clean, out of ignorance they often lived in conditions that would appall and nauseate even the messiest of their modern counterparts. It was common for rubbish, including food and animal wastes, to build up on the dirt floors of homes, for example. People swept them out from time to time; but many of the bacteria that multiplied in such wastes remained. The discarded rubbish ended up in roadside or backyard piles, which grew larger over time and remained breeding grounds for germs. Archaeologists have found the village dump just outside the residential area of Deir el-Medina as well as a dump measuring nearly four hundred by five hundred feet near the larger city of Amarna.

which during the day he uses for fishing, and at night fixes up round his bed and creeps in under it before he goes to sleep.[28]

Other pests that regularly and widely infested homes and other human habitations included bedbugs, rats, mice, and snakes. In the ruins of ancient Egyptian homes archaeologists have found many rat holes, which the residents tried to block by stuffing them with rags, as well as numerous rat skeletons. Rats not only fouled human food supplies and bit babies, but

Healing Through Magic

However they got sick, the Egyptians tried to combat illness and disease using a combination of methods, some of them fairly effective, but others completely ineffective. The ineffective ones employed some form of magic, which was a central part of the Egyptian religious belief system.

Almost all people, regardless of social class, age, or gender, wore or carried amulets, necklaces, figurines, or other objects thought to have magical properties that protected the owner.

Magic also played a major role in Egyptian medical practice. Some doctors were priests, but others were laypersons; and among the lay physicians were large numbers who used only magic to treat their patients. (The other lay physicians and the priest-doctors employed surgery and herbal therapy, but they also resorted to magic when they thought it appropriate.) In fact, many surviving Egyptian medical documents contain magic spells intended to ward off disease and other ailments. The physician might recite the spell himself. But he also often advised patients to recite the magical words repeatedly until they felt better (sort of the ancient magician's equivalent of a modern doctor advising someone to "take this pill four times a day until the symptoms subside"). The following example calls on the goddess Isis to ward off a certain illness (and hopefully any others that might later afflict the patient):

> May Isis heal me even as she healed [her son] Horus of the pains which his brother Seth had inflicted on him when he killed his brother Osiris! O Isis, you great enchantress, heal me, deliver me from all evil, bad . . . things, from demoniacal and deadly diseases and pollutions of all sorts that rush upon me, as you did deliver and release your son Horus![29]

Sometimes the doctors or patients combined the magic spells with traditional home remedies. To eliminate a headache, for example, one recited a certain incantation while mixing together fish products with onions, honey, and other ingredients and then rubbing this mixture on the head. Or if a doctor wanted to get rid of the cataracts in his patient's eyes, he mixed a turtle's brain with honey and rubbed the concoction on the eyes while saying a spell that included these words:

A tomb carving shows Hesire, chief doctor and dentist to the pharaoh Djoser.

There is a shouting in the southern sky in the darkness. There is an uproar in the northern sky. The hall of pillars falls into the waters. . . . I lift up your necks. I fasten what has been cut from you in its place. I lead you forth to drive away the god of fevers and all possible deadly arts.[30]

More Rational Medical Approaches

Egyptian doctors often also took the more practical approach of administering home remedies that did not involve magic. Many such cures were committed to writing on papyrus rolls. One, which modern scholars call the Ebers Medical Papyrus, dating from the early New Kingdom, features a remedy for severe indigestion:

Take a casserole [dish], half-filled with water [and] half-filled with onions. Let it stand for four days. See that it does not become dry. After it has stood moist, beat to a froth one-fourth of the third part of the contents of this vessel, and let him who suffers from the vomiting drink it for four days so that he may become well.[31]

The same compilation of remedies includes one to eliminate itching:

[Take] cyperus-from-the-meadow [a local herb], onion-meal, incense, [and] wild date-juice. [Mix these together] and apply to the scurvy [irritated] place. Look to it because this is the true remedy. It was found among the proven remedies in the temple of the god Osiris. It is a remedy which drives away the scurf [irritation] in every limb of a person. Yes, it heals at once![32]

For serious wounds that occurred in warfare or accidents, many Egyptian doctors used methods not all that different

Pictured are fragments of the Kahun Medical Papyrus, which contains information about pregnancy and other women's medical issues.

from those employed by their modern counterparts. These included using splints to help reset broken bones and needle and thread to sew up cuts and deep wounds. Several such procedures are outlined in fair detail in the so-called *Book of Surgery* (today known as the Edwin Smith Medical Papyrus). The copy that survives was made in the 1600s B.C., shortly before the advent of the New Kingdom; however, scholars believe that most of the contents date from several centuries before, possibly as far back as the early Old Kingdom. The following example offers advice on how to treat a deep wound over the eyebrow.

If you examine a man having a wound in the top of the eyebrow, penetrating to the bone, you should palpate [examine by touching] the wound and draw together for him his gash with stitching. You should say concerning him: "One having a wound in his eyebrow. An ailment which I will treat." Now, after you have stitched it, you should bind fresh meat upon it the first day. If you find that the stitching of his wound is loose, you should draw it together for him with two strips of plaster, and you should treat it with grease and honey every day until he recovers.[33]

Egyptian medicine was also strongly preoccupied with traditionally female conditions and ailments. The Kahun Medical Papyrus (dating from circa 2000 B.C.), for instance, contains information about diagnosing pregnancy. It also offers remedies for women suffering from toothaches and abdominal pain during pregnancy as well as methods of contraception.

It is unclear how often these and other examples of Egyptian healing worked and to what degree. But it seems certain that they were effective often enough for doctors to continue using them for many centuries. If nothing else, they demonstrate a sincere desire to reduce human suffering. Combined with the Egyptians' preoccupation with personal hygiene and grooming, they paint a picture of a highly civilized, humane, and caring people who did the utmost with the minimal amount of technology and scientific knowledge available to them.

Chapter Four

THE WORLD'S BREADBASKET: FOODS AND DIET

Because so much of Egypt consists of arid deserts, and also because of descriptions of Egyptian famines in the Bible, many people envision ancient Egypt as an impoverished land nearly always on the brink of starvation. In reality, nothing could be further from the truth. With only occasional exceptions, the ancient Egyptians were a well-fed people with a fairly varied diet. According to James Romano, abundant evidence "suggests that even the humblest peasants could find sufficient nourishment, if only through fishing, hunting, fowling [trapping birds], and gathering."[34]

Moreover, most of the time these methods of acquiring food were secondary to the practice of agriculture, which the Egyptians engaged in on a huge scale. Egypt usually produced so much food, in fact, that several ancient peoples, including the Greeks and the Romans, viewed it as the breadbasket of the Mediterranean world. (A large proportion of the grain consumed in Roman Italy from the first century B.C. on was imported from Egypt.) Only when the Nile River failed to produce its annual floods (which irrigated farmers' fields) did the volume of food production in Egypt temporarily decline. And even then, emergency distribution of surplus grain stored in stone granaries made famine a rarity.

The fact that the ancient Egyptians normally had plenty of food is even more impressive when one considers the large number of mouths that needed to be fed. Though much of Egypt does indeed contain vast tracts of arid wastelands, the small green portions watered by the Nile supported a hefty population by ancient standards. An important ecological study published in 1976 by noted geographer Karl Butzer estimated that ancient Egypt supported a population of close to a million people at the time it became a nation (ca. 3100 B.C.). That number had risen to at least 1.6 million by the height of the Old Kingdom (ca.

A detail from the Palestrina Mosaic, dating from the second century A.D., shows farmers during the flood season.

2500 B.C.); 3 million by the peak of the New Kingdom (ca. 1250 B.C.); and 5 million by the end of the Ptolemaic Period (ca. 30 B.C.). By comparison, Greece had an estimated population of little more than 2 million in Ptolemaic times.

Bread—Egypt's Staple Food

In general, the kinds of foods people consumed in ancient Egypt depended on their wealth and social class. As has been true nearly everywhere throughout history, the wealthy could afford a more varied diet than the poor, even when the poor had plenty to eat. Still, both rich and poor Egyptians ate large amounts of the country's staple food—bread. Following the advent of settled agriculture in the Nile Valley in late Stone Age times, grains, especially wheat, long remained the chief crops. Well before the ages of the pharaohs, back when Egypt was made up of many disunited villages and towns, people learned to grind the grain into flour, transform the flour into dough, and bake the dough into bread.

During most of the centuries of pharaonic Egypt, wheat and other grains were crushed in a primitive, labor-intensive fashion. The men of a family placed the harvested grain on flat limestone blocks and applied stone pestles (rounded grinding tools). When they were finished, they gave the semicrushed grain to the family women. The women crushed the grain a second time using spherical stone rollers. Large millstones rotated by the muscle power of animals or humans were not introduced into Egypt until the Ptolemaic Period. The result of these primitive grinding methods was that Egyptian flour tended to be quite

A wooden carving from the Old Kingdom shows a woman grinding grain for bread, one of Egypt's staple foods.

course and grainy; modern studies reveal that it contained particles of quartz, mica, and other minerals, as well as many partially crushed and uncrushed grains. The bread made from such flour would best be described as crunchy. (Examination of human remains shows that these abrasive particles did considerable damage to people's teeth over time.)

To make dough, people added water to the flour, along with varying amounts of milk, yeast, spices, salt, and eggs. (As is true today, the exact recipes varied from place to place and time to time. At least twenty kinds of bread existed in the Old Kingdom and up to fifty kinds in the New Kingdom.) After they mixed the dough, they allowed it to sit for a while and rise (thanks to the action of the yeast).

Then they baked the dough. In the earliest times, this was accomplished simply by placing it on a thin slab of stone or pottery and holding the slab over an open fire. By the advent of the Old Kingdom, pottery bread molds were in use. One first preheated the mold in a fire, then removed it, greased the inside with fat, and inserted the wad of dough. The pottery's built-up heat baked the dough into bread. Larger bread ovens—consisting of a fire box in the bottom, a stone grating to hold the bread in the middle, and a dome-shaped oven space at the top—came into use in the Middle Kingdom. All of these bread-making methods and ovens were confined to home and other localized use until the beginning of the New Kingdom. Only then did commercial bakeries serving the community become common. (An exception that existed as early as the Old Kingdom consisted of large baking facilities set up in temporary workers' villages near major construction sites. Such bakeries have been excavated near the great pyramids at Giza.)

Other Basic Foods

In addition to various kinds of bread, the Egyptians ate large amounts of meat, vegetables, and fruit. Meat consumption seems to have been higher among the well-to-do than among people of average means, but the latter enjoyed plenty of meat during religious holidays and other special occasions. From the Old Kingdom on, meat came mostly from domesticated livestock. By that time hunting had become more of a recreational activity than a necessity and supplied only marginal amounts of meat. The chief kinds of meat came from cattle, goats, sheep, pigs, and several species of bird, including geese, pigeons, herons, and pelicans. (Because of local religious and social taboos, pork was eaten only in certain areas of the country.)

Fish was another kind of meat eaten in ancient Egypt (although local taboos and superstitions caused some people to avoid certain species of fish). Catfish, perch, and mullet were among the many species of Nile fish harvested by fishermen. Many fishermen scaled and cleaned the fish in their boats right after catching them. Fish that were not eaten immediately were salted to preserve them, and during the country's Greek and Roman periods large amounts of salted fish were exported to other Mediterranean lands.

To go with their bread, meat, or fish, the Egyptians cultivated a wide variety of vegetables and fruits. The vegetables included lettuce, beets, turnips, radishes, chickpeas, lentils, beans, leeks, cucumbers, and garlic, among others. (People used garlic not only to flavor food but also for health reasons, as they thought that the odor of garlic helped ward off disease.) Sweet onions were especially popular. An additional use for onions was placing them in the eye sockets, armpits, and body cavities of mummies, probably based on the belief that the onions' pungent odor would help the deceased to breathe in the afterlife. Among the most common fruits consumed in pharaonic Egypt were figs, dates, raisins, grapes, plums, and watermelons. Other popular fruits, including bananas, oranges, peaches, mangoes, and lemons, were not introduced into the country until the Greek and Roman eras or later.

To flavor and enliven their food, the Egyptians used a number of spices and other additives still common today. Among them was salt. Again because of religious

A tomb painting depicts a rich collection of foodstuffs for use by the deceased in the afterlife.

taboos (in this case involving the evil god Seth, who was associated with the sea), sea salt was viewed as unclean. So people got their salt from mineral deposits in selected spots in the desert. For sweeteners, members of the upper classes used honey, while the poor mainly used date juice, called *bener*, meaning "sweet" or "pleasant." Although the ancient Egyptian word for butter has not yet been identified, scholars point to images in paintings of people handling what appears to be butter; so it is likely that many Egyptians used butter as a spread, as is common today.

Cooking and Food Preparation

It is possible that the Egyptians also used butter for cooking. It is certain that they did use certain fats and oils for frying meat and vegetables. They distinguished between animal fats—collectively termed *adj*—and vegetable oils—called *merhet*. Words for twenty-one different kinds of *merhet* have been identified, including those derived from flax, sesame, and radish seeds; castor-oil plants; olives; and horseradish trees, the latter being particularly prized. (For a long

The remains of a kitchen in a well-to-do family's villa include two cooking facilities—a stone hearth (left) and a cylindrical oven for baking.

time olives and olive oil were imported from other lands, especially Palestine and Greece. Some local olive cultivation began in the New Kingdom, but the industry did not become large in Egypt until the Ptolemaic Period, when the Faiyum became a major olive-producing region.)

To cook with these fats or oils, a person placed them, along with the food, in a large pottery saucepan, which had one or two long handles. He or she suspended the pan, either by hand or on a stone or metal tripod, over an open fire or a "stove." In the average Egyptian home, a stove consisted of a small stone hearth or a cylindrical baked-clay enclosure standing about three feet high. Each held a fire that heated the stone or ceramic surfaces until they were hot enough to cook on. An opening in the bottom of the hearth or stove created a draft to keep oxygen flowing to the fire as well as to allow for easy removal of accumulated ashes. Wealthier homes often cooked using metal braziers (bowl-like containers) similar to modern portable charcoal grills. In fact, to fuel their cooking fires members of the upper classes used charcoal or wood. In contrast, the poor more often used dried reeds, straw, or animal droppings.

Preparation of the food that was cooked in these devices was done with a few simple utensils, including stone or metal knives and wooden ladles, stirrers, and whisks. Like the saucepans, mixing bowls in the average home were made of inexpensive but sturdy pottery. Some richer homes supplemented these with metal containers.

But in both rich and poor homes food storage jars were made of pottery and kept in shallow cellars under or near the kitchen area (the equivalent of today's closet pantries). In an average home the wife or mother, who did most of the cooking, monitored the storage jars closely; when supplies were getting low, she or another family member made sure the necessary shopping or foraging was done. In wealthier homes, where servants did the food preparation, there was an ever-present danger of filching from the food storage. "To guard against petty thievery by servants," Romano explains,

> wealthy Egyptians would place over the mouth of the storage vessel a pottery saucer that they tied in place by knotting a linen cloth around the jar neck. They covered the knot with a mass of clay or wax stamped with the name of the owner. A would-be thief could not disturb the contents of the jar without first destroying the seal.[35]

Popular Beverages

Various beverages were also stored in ceramic jars in the kitchen area. Some Egyptians drank milk, especially when they were young. Some evidence suggests that adult milk consumption was highest among rural farmers, who had the most direct access to fresh milk from livestock. With no way to refrigerate it, milk could not be shipped and stored for weeks or more, as it is today, so people in cities tended to drink less of it.

Small wooden figures from the Middle Kingdom show workers wetting grain that will be crushed and fermented to produce beer.

However, people in both the cities and the countryside drank a great deal of beer, perhaps more than in any other ancient land. This was partly because the Egyptians made their beer from wheat and other grains, which were the chief crops and therefore a readily available raw material. Another factor may have been the high alcohol content of ancient Egyptian beer—between 6 and 8 percent, which is about twice as high as in most modern beers. Many people may have enjoyed the feeling of well-being that came from slight intoxication.

To make what might be called the national drink, the family women, who did most of the brewing, began with bushels of grain and jars of water. According to Eugen Strouhal:

The grain would be soaked in water for a day, rolled out and left to dry, then wetted again, crushed and trodden in large vats with yeast added. When fermentation was well advanced, the mash [was] filtered through a sieve [strainer] or piece of cloth. . . . Finally, the [liquid] was seasoned with spices, dates, mandrake, safflower, or other additives—hops [used in modern beer making] was unknown. . . . Before being drunk, beer was poured through a sieve or fine-meshed cloth to remove remains of the additives and other impurities.[36]

The Egyptians also drank wine. But it was more expensive than beer, so it was consumed mainly by the well-to-do or by the poor on special occasions. Tomb paintings from both the Old and New kingdoms show the typical local wine-making process. Men tossed large bunches of grapes into a big wooden vat and crushed them by trampling them with their feet (a technique still used in many parts of the world today). While crushing the grapes, the men held onto ropes suspended above the vat so that if they slipped they would not fall into the messy mash. The juice

A painting from a New Kingdom tomb depicts men trampling grapes in a big vat, a wine-making technique still used in some places today.

This painting from an Eighteenth-dynasty tomb shows men and women attending a banquet in the home of a well-to-do host.

from this mash trickled through a wooden trough or pipe at the bottom and into a wooden or pottery vessel resting below. After filtering the juice through a sieve, the wine makers stored it in vats and allowed it to ferment. Finally, they drained the wine into big pottery jars, and those who could afford it stored it in their home, palace, or temple kitchens.

Dining Customs

Storage areas for food and drink were obviously most active shortly before and during mealtimes. With occasional exceptions, most Egyptians—namely those of average or below-average means—ate twice a day, once around sunrise and again around sunset. Sometimes people had a small snack, such as a piece of fruit or a small chunk of bread, during the course of the day. In contrast, well-to-do people tended to eat full-fledged lunches (or brunches).

During a meal, people of lesser means generally sat or squatted on the floor around a low table made of a simple slab of wood or stone. Those in better-off homes sat on chairs or stools fairly similar to modern ones, often around circular tables decorated with flowers. Whether rich or poor, however, diners did not use forks, spoons, or other utensils. Instead, everyone, even the pharaohs and their royal relatives, ate with their hands, which inspired the common custom of washing one's hands several times during the course of a meal. Many people also rinsed out their mouths with mineral salts at least once or twice while eating.

Such cleanliness rituals were most pronounced at banquets given by royal and wealthy individuals. At such gatherings, servants walked from table to table carrying pitchers of water and bowls. At appropriate moments they poured water over guests' hands and into the bowls, then emptied the bowls outside. Meanwhile, other servants supplied the guests with a wide range of elaborately prepared dishes, including many containing meat and fowl. As they ate, the diners enjoyed entertainment in the form of musicians and female dancers.

Eating and Drinking Too Much

One seemingly inevitable consequence of upper-class dining customs—eating big lunches and consuming large amounts of fancy food at both lunch and dinner—was overindulgence. Artistic and other evidence shows that average Egyptians were almost always on the lean side. This makes sense for people who ate only two meals a day and performed some measure of physical labor on a regular basis. In richer circles, by contrast, where people ate more and did little or no work, corpulent (overweight)

A Strange Dining Custom

Some of the customs surrounding wealthy dinner parties in ancient Egypt appear exceedingly strange to modern observers. The Greek historian Herodotus recorded one such odd custom, which incorporated potent imagery of the dead, in his Histories, *written after his extended stay in Egypt.*

When the rich give a party and the meal is finished, a man carries round amongst the guests a wooden image of a corpse in a coffin, carved and painted to look as much like the real thing as possible, and anything from eighteen inches to three feet long. He shows it to each guest in turn, and says, "Look upon this body as you drink and enjoy yourself. For you will be just like that when you are dead."

individuals were more common. Some were even obese.

Ancient Egyptians often viewed being overweight as a sign of high social station; therefore, it was accepted and even envied rather than seen in a negative light. On the flip side, as remains true today, overweight people were more prone to suffering from maladies such as heart disease, urinary stones, and diabetes. (It is unclear whether the Egyptians connected the incidence of these problems with overeating and excess weight.)

Some Egyptians also overindulged in intoxicating drinks. Though people in all social classes probably did so from time to time, drunkenness was probably most pronounced at rich banquets in which the guests had access to huge amounts of beer and especially high-alcohol-content wine. A painting in one tomb shows a woman at a party gesturing to a servant, with the following inscription: "Bring me 18 goblets of wine. Can't you see that I'm trying to get drunk? My throat is as dry as dust!"[37] Other tomb paintings show well-to-do banqueters vomiting or being carried away by their friends after drinking too much.

But although such behavior may have been common at such gatherings, society in general seems to have frowned on it. The *Instruction of Any*, a work well regarded by educated people in ancient Egypt, warns about the ill effects of drunkenness:

Don't indulge in drinking [too much] beer, lest you [get drunk and] utter evil speech and don't know what you're saying. If [your intoxicated state causes] you [to] fall and hurt your body, none will hold out a hand to you. Your companions in the drinking stand up saying: "Out with the drunk!" If one comes to seek you and talk with you, one finds you lying [in a drunken stupor] on the ground, as if you were a child.[38]

Passages like this one, along with other evidence, show that many of the problems associated with food and drink today are far from new. The Egyptians dealt with them on a regular basis, part of the complex fabric of daily life on the banks of the ancient Nile.

Chapter Five

IN THE WISE MAN'S FOOTSTEPS: EDUCATION AND LEARNING

Education was extremely important to the ancient Egyptians, even though the vast majority of them could neither read nor write. At first glance this might seem to be both illogical and an oxymoron (a statement of two ideas that contradict each other). But such a judgment is invariably colored by modern concepts and practices, which define education mainly in terms of formal schooling that emphasizes reading, writing, and book learning. A few ancient Egyptians did acquire such skills. But the majority who were illiterate learned vocational and social skills, as well as moral training, in their homes. In Egyptian society, parents were viewed as teachers who were just as important as the ones who taught in schools.

Thus, in the general sense society did not make education an institution separate from home life and upbringing, as is the case today. Rather, all Egyptians recognized the value of and received some form of instruction. It might take the form of a girl learning spinning and weaving from her mother, a boy learning his father's trade, or a boy learning to read and write in a formalized school-like setting. Along with moral and ethical training imparted by their elders, all of these learning situations were seen as forms of education. Most of those who were illiterate and never attended formal schools usually did not think of themselves as underprivileged. In their view, and indeed in society's view as well, it was part of the natural, traditional order for different people to learn different sorts of things in different ways.

Education in the Home

As part of this natural, traditional order, up to a certain age all children learned from their parents. That age varied according to such factors as the child's gender, the family's status and situation, and the father's profession. In families of average means, for example, girls received training

A governess holds a young pharaoh in her lap in this wall painting. Learning always began at home.

in skills such as making clothes and cooking during early childhood. But as a rule this was the extent of their education. It is doubtful that poor girls learned to read and write, although there may have been occasional exceptions. If so, their parents taught them, for they did not attend formal schools.

In contrast, girls in wealthy homes often also learned to dance, sing, and play musi-cal instruments. They generally did not use these skills to make a living since they did not have to work, but they learned them as social refinements expected of women in the upper classes. It appears that a few of the girls brought up in well-to-do homes learned to read and write. The evidence for this takes the form of their signatures on various documents and a few surviving letters that seem to have been written by women to women. (It is of course possible that the women had men write and read these letters for them.) However, these cases are fairly rare, so female literacy was likely not widespread.

A majority of boys and men were illiterate, too, although the number of literate boys far exceeded that of girls who could read. For the most part, if the family was of average or lower than average means there was little chance a boy would receive a formal education. Usually he learned and thereby perpetuated his father's trade, often as an apprentice. As noted scholar T.G.H. James points out, this was advantageous for the community. "Continuity was achieved in skills" vital to the community, "in the protection of craft secrets," and in "the special advantages enjoyed by individual families."[39] Thus, by teaching his son his trade, a village carpenter might ensure that his family would continue to maintain its economic and social standing in the community. And the community would continue to benefit by having a competent person to take care of its carpentry needs.

For the common people in Egypt, parents and home life also played the key roles in developing their children's social skills and moral compass. "Parents familiarized their children with their ideas about the world," Eugen Strouhal writes, "with their religious outlook, with their ethical principles, with correct behavior toward others and toward the supernatural beings in whom everyone believed. They taught them about folk rituals and so forth."[40] In these ways, most young Egyptians received the essentials of learning at home and in the local community without feeling the need for formal schooling or any regret over not achieving literacy.

The Value of Formal Education and Literacy

That does not mean that the few who did get formal educations and became literate were not more privileged than or did not feel superior to those who could not read and write. On the one hand, formal schooling and literacy could provide a path to jobs in government service, which brought considerable money, social status, and power to those involved. "Few jobs of any consequence in the state could satisfactorily be performed without the capabilities of reading and writing," scholar Rosalie David points out.

A high official would, it must be granted, have relied on his trained staff to prepare documents, and he may also have had a clerk to read out whatever written material needed to be consulted on occasion. But the high official, if he were worthy of his position and

not prepared to be at the mercy of his . . . assistants, would have at least have been able to read.[41]

Clearly, such jobs were out of reach and out of the question for poor illiterate peasants.

On the other hand, young people who learned to read and write could also choose to become teachers themselves. Many school students observed and envied their teachers' respected social position and

The Satisfying Path of Learning

This excerpt from the Satire of Trades *(translated in John L. Foster's* Ancient Egyptian Literature*) extols the personal value and satisfaction that could come from higher learning.*

Now, it is good to study many things, [so] that you [will] learn the wisdom of great men. Thus you can help to educate the children of the people while you walk according to the wise man's footsteps. The scribe is seen as listening and obeying, and the listening develops into satisfaction. Hold fast [always remember] the words which hearken to these things, as your own footsteps hurry, and while you are on your journey you need never hide your heart. Step out on the path of learning—[for] the friends of mankind are your company.

comfortable lifestyle. From a physical standpoint, this special class of literate individuals—the scribes—had an easier life than farmers, craftsmen, soldiers, and construction workers, who performed some form of hard physical labor on a daily basis. So many of the few highly educated individuals in society tended to urge their sons and students to become scribes. In this way, David says, they might "escape the toil associated with all other trades. Describing how all other work is subject

A scribe holds a queen's daughter in this granite sculpture. Scribes were Egypt's principal teachers.

to supervision and its own hardships," documents penned by scribes extolled "the excellence and status of the scribe's profession."[42] The famous Middle Kingdom document known as the *Satire of Trades* summed up this view while emphasizing the importance of education itself:

> You must give yourself whole-heartedly to learning [to read and write], [and thereby] discover what will save you from the drudgery of underlings. Nothing is so valuable as [formal] education; it is a bridge over troubled water.... Let me urge you to love learning more than your mother; have its perfections enter your mind. It is more distinguished than any other occupation. There is nothing [else] like it upon Earth![43]

Schools and Teachers

The scribes and their privileged students were not part of a widespread public education system like those familiar in most countries today. Indeed, Egypt had neither a structured educational system nor even buildings erected specifically to serve solely as schools. Instead, higher education (the goal of which was to teach reading, writing, and other highly specialized skills) was a private affair and centered around the scribes themselves. For example, the royal palace employed a number of scribes to teach the pharaoh's children, along with the children of his vizier (his chief administrator), and a few other high officials. Lessons took place in various places within the palace and on the surrounding grounds.

Although detailed evidence is lacking, it appears that scribes also held vocational classes within the individual departments of the government. In other words, the officials in charge of the military, foreign diplomacy, large-scale engineering projects, tax collection, and so forth needed trained assistants and operatives. Over time some of these assistants would gain promotions and eventually some of them would replace the top officials when they retired or died. Some of the training of these subordinates was done by the top officials themselves in a sort of apprenticeship system. In fact, it was often very similar to the situation in which village craftsmen taught their sons a trade, as many state officials groomed their own sons for government service. However, the high officials were so busy with their jobs that they often needed help in teaching their sons and other assistants. And so, they hired scribes to provide both basic and specialized instruction.

Another common educational setting in which scribes conducted classes was the religious temple. Apparently such instruction took place in a section called the House of Life, which was devoted mainly to collecting and copying literature (by hand), including hymns and stories relating to the gods. Not surprisingly, many of the students who attended these temple schools later became priests. But the subjects taught were not solely religious in nature, and some of the students in these schools went on to become government officials, military officers, or scribes.

Prayers Used as School Texts

Among the texts commonly used by students in ancient Egypt's scribal schools were prayers to the gods. These served the dual purpose of giving the students acceptable material to copy while learning to write and further strengthening the religious piety already instilled in them by their parents. This example (quoted in volume 2 of Miriam Lichtheim's Ancient Egyptian Literature*) praises the highly revered sun god, Amun-Ra.*

Amun-Ra, who first was king [of Egypt in a distant past age], the god of earliest time, the vizier [superintendent] of the poor. He does not take bribes from the guilty, he does not speak to the [false] witness, he does not look at him who promises [things but breaks those promises]. Amun judges the land with his fingers. He speaks to the heart. [In the afterlife] he judges the guilty, he assigns him [the guilty man] to the east [a bad place where he will live in misery forever], the righteous [man] to the west [where he will meet the god Osiris and enter the Underworld, where his life will be comfortable].

Not all teachers plied their trade in major institutions like the palace, government, and temples. It appears that an unknown number worked in small communities and villages, where they tutored the sons of local officials or anyone else who could afford to pay them. It is unknown what form the payment took, but most likely people gave a teacher food, lodging, slaves, and/or various gifts in exchange for his services. Also uncertain is who these community teachers were and where they received their own education. Some were probably local people who had found some way to get into a temple school and had eventually returned to the community. Such private teachers existed in the workers' village at Deir el-Medina, though no evidence of a formal school in the town has yet been found.

Methods of Instruction

Children were taught to read and write by rote memorization accomplished by repeated recitation or writing of selected passages. This method is still used in most Muslim religious schools (the madrassas, which originated in the twelfth century A.D.) in Egypt and a number of other Middle Eastern countries today. Typically students recited aloud short passages from well-known texts over and over until they had memorized them almost word for word and could recognize and understand all the words. In another approach, the teacher dictated sections of a text and the students tried their best to write down the words using correct spelling and grammar. The teacher would correct the writings and the process would be repeated, each time hopefully producing fewer errors.

Another aspect of rote learning in ancient Egypt was the repeated compiling of lists. These could be lists of grammatical rules or verb forms, such as the Egyptian words for *I am, he is, we are, they are,* and so on. Or they might be lists of towns in Egypt, or foreign peoples, or the former pharaohs of Egypt. The latter, now known as the "king lists," were customarily inscribed on official stelae and palace and temple walls. But archaeologists found a version of a king list at Deir el-Medina that had been used by a local teacher named Qen-her-khepseh-ef for his students' rote memory exercises.

The writing media the students used to compile such lists were of a few basic types. Perhaps most common were ostraka, either pieces of broken pottery or small flakes of limestone. Pottery shards could be found in large numbers in town rubbish heaps; and limestone chips were abundant in quarries and construction sites. The student either scratched the letters into the surface with a sharp object or applied black paint using a pen consisting of a simple river reed with a frayed tip. The painted ones could sometimes be reused by washing off the paint. The rest were discarded.

Another fairly common writing medium used by students was a slate or tablet made of wood. Such boards were generally made of wood, often sycamore, covered with gesso (a type of plaster). Modern scholars believe that students wiped the boards clean and reused them many times before they wore out. In fact, some surviving examples have faint traces of older writing visible beneath later texts. When a board did wear out, it could be resurfaced with a fresh layer of plaster.

Less commonly, students wrote on papyrus parchment. And when they did it was usually a piece that had been used before. They either rubbed off the older writing or covered it over with a thin layer of paint or plaster. The reason why students rarely used new papyrus sheets was because such sheets required a number of time-consuming steps to make and were therefore moderately expensive. Still another writing medium, consisting of waxed tablets that students inscribed by means of a metal stylus (a pointed tool), was introduced by the Greeks during Ptolemaic times.

Discipline

By whatever methods Egyptian students learned, their teachers had to be disciplinarians as well as instructors. That ancient Egyptian children could be as lazy, bored with school, and mischievous as their mod-

Common writing media included the wooden slate (below) and pottery shards called ostraka (inset).

ern counterparts is proven by numerous passages from surviving documents. Among the most revealing are a series of statements and writing exercises compiled by the scribal teachers themselves—today referred to as the *Miscellanies*. One shows what a strict teacher expected from his students:

> [You are in] school with the children of high officials, to teach and instruct you in this office which [when you are older] will lead [you] to power and authority. . . . [Your teacher orders: "Be] prompt in [getting to] your place [in the classroom]! Write [your exercises] in front of your fellows. Put your hand to your clothes [i.e., make sure you look tidy]." . . . Don't be lazy! . . . Write with your hand; recite with your mouth; accept advice. Let yourself not be tired [bored?]; and pass no day in laziness, or it will be misery for your body. Enter into the ways of your teacher, and obey his instructions![44]

The phrase "it will be misery for your body" was a polite, indirect reference to the application of corporal punishment. Other passages from the *Miscellanies* are much more direct in threatening rule breakers with physical punishment. "Pass no day in laziness," a scribe named Amenemope warns, "or you will be beaten. The ear of a lad happens to be on his back. He listens when he is beaten. . . . I will make you a man, you bad boy! Consider that!"[45] There is no way to know if all teachers resorted to physical violence to maintain discipline; but the large number of passages threat-ening beatings, like those above, suggest that this form of discipline was endemic in Egypt's educational system throughout ancient times.

Curriculum and Teaching Aids

Such a primitive and heavy-handed approach to disciplining students rather starkly contrasts with the reasoned, humane tone of most of the texts the students used in their studies. A large proportion of the passages they repeatedly recited and copied came from a branch of Egyptian literature now referred to as wisdom literature. In particular they absorbed examples from the wisdom genre known as instruction. The most common form of literary instruction was a lecture given by a father to his son or by a high official to a subordinate. And among the more popular examples passed down from generation to generation were the *Satire of Trades*, *Maxims of Ptahhotep*, and the *Instruction of Any*. These works dealt with themes such as justice, honesty, and hard work. In addition, as David points out, they

> counsel caution in speech, prudence in friendship, and good behavior in the houses of others and at the table. They recommend modesty and specify correct behavior toward peers, superiors, and inferiors. The advice is practical and seeks to ensure advancement in life and to promote the skills required in good leaders.[46]

By using such popular and revered literature as the mainstay of the school curriculum, therefore, the scribal schools accomplished two goals simultaneously. On the one hand they provided the students with plenty of well-written practice material. On the other, and perhaps ultimately more importantly, they tried to instill a sense of justice, honesty, humanity, and simple good breeding in the country's future social and political leaders.

This may well explain, at least in part, the relatively high quality of the country's leaders over the course of many centuries. The pharaohs were absolute monarchs who could easily have abused their huge powers and imposed cruel tyrannical rule. But though a few may have ruled harshly, the evidence suggests that the vast majority of these rulers were humane, enlightened, constructive, or at least well meaning. One cannot dismiss the possibility that the genteel, tolerant tone and message of the literary instructions memorized in schools helped to shape the ethical vision of the country and its leaders.

Some of Ptahhotep's advice, for example, not only urges tolerance for others but even has a democratic undercurrent in the way it calls for decent treatment of the poor, weak, and underprivileged: "If you meet a . . . poor man, not your equal, do not attack him because he is weak, [but rather] let him alone. . . . Wretched is he who injures a poor man." Ptahhotep even counsels the high-placed person to respect an underling's intellect and opinions: "Don't be proud of your knowledge. Consult [both] the ignorant and wise. . . .

Students Advised to Show Restraint

Among the literary instructions used in scribal schools in generation after generation was that attributed to a man named Amenemope, likely composed in the early New Kingdom. Through the process of repetition and rote memory, many of the students surely absorbed some of his advice. The following example (quoted in W.K. Simpson's anthology of Egyptian writings), urges restraint when dealing with testy or angry people.

Do not get into a quarrel with the argumentative man, nor incite him with words; proceed cautiously before an opponent, and give way to an adversary. Sleep on it before speaking, for a storm [of loud or violent reaction] comes forth like fire in hay. The hotheaded man in his appointed time— may you be restrained before him. Leave him to himself, and God will know how to answer him. If you spend your life with these things in your heart, your children shall behold them [and grow up with the same good values].

Good speech is more hidden than greenstone, yet may be found among [poor] maids [working] at the grindstone."[47]

This and other popular instructions used as teaching aids also strongly stressed justice for the poor and helpless, not simply for the privileged and powerful. A striking

In his popular maxims, the sage Ptahhotep, seen in this bas-relief, urged people to be tolerant and respectful to the underprivileged.

example comes from a New kingdom document—the *Instruction of Amenemope:*

> Beware of stealing from a miserable man and of raging against the cripple. . . . Do not covet the property of the poor [man], nor hunger for his bread. . . . If you find a large debt against a poor man [i.e., if a poor man owes you a lot of money], make it into three parts. Release [forgive or cancel] two of them and let one remain. . . . [Thereafter] you pass the night in sound sleep [knowing that you have done a good deed]. . . . Do not jeer at a blind man, nor tease a dwarf. Neither interfere with the condition of a cripple. Do not taunt a man who is [in an unfortunate state because of] the hand of God.[48]

Maintaining Harmony and Order

Thus, education was a cornerstone of Egyptian society on more than one level. First, it ensured that sons would follow in their fathers' footsteps and maintain the integrity and usefulness of the common trades so vital to society's normal functioning. It also created a literate class that, though small, made record keeping, literature, and complex governmental administration possible. And finally, the educational system created a moral tradition and atmosphere that bred humane rulers, social courtesy, and decent treatment of the poor and underprivileged. In a very real sense, that system perpetuated society's moral code, which Strouhal effectively summarizes:

> Virtue will be rewarded for [the following] reasons: Behave justly toward your god, your king, your superiors, and your inferiors too; in return you will enjoy health, long life, and respect. When judging the dead, god will deal with you in accordance with your past conduct. Those you leave behind, too, will be glad to acknowledge your good deeds by . . . bringing gifts to [your tomb to] ensure you life eternal. The supreme goal of the Egyptian moral system [stressed by parents, teachers, and authority figures alike] was to help maintain harmony and order in the world created by god and maintained by the king.[49]

Chapter Six

MAINTAINING MA'AT: CRIME AND PUNISHMENT

The moral precepts stressed in the Egyptian educational system were in large part inspired by and designed to perpetuate *ma'at*, a concept sometimes associated with a goddess of the same name (Ma'at). This somewhat indefinite term has no exact or simple English translation. To the Egyptians it could mean "order," "harmony," "correctness," "justice," or a combination of two or more of these things. Noted Egyptologist Ian Shaw calls it "the common sense view of right or wrong as defined by the social norms of the day."[50]

Egypt's loose system of justice was also based on *ma'at*. The Egyptians did not have a complex set of written laws and rules like those formulated in ancient Rome and modern democracies like Britain and the United States. As far as modern scholars can tell, Egypt had no formal law code such as those of the Babylonian ruler Hammurabi and Athenian lawgiver Solon. Instead, most laws, court procedures, verdicts, and punishments seem to have been based on custom and precedent. The judges in a particular case looked back at how similar past cases had been handled and, aided by common sense and a desire to maintain *ma'at*, rendered their opinions and sentences.

An Unusually Civil Society

Egypt could maintain order and legal fairness without an elaborate written legal code because its society was an unusually civil one compared to most others, both ancient and modern. Indeed, from the earliest times civility and common courtesy were highly encouraged and venerated among people of all social classes. Typical of societal attitudes about proper human interaction are those expressed in this passage from the *Instruction of Amenemope*:

> Avoid demeaning the already miserable by any show of strength against

the weak. Do not raise your hand against the aging, nor criticize the conversations of the great. Do not formulate your messages in an abrasive manner, nor envy one who does. Do not raise a cry against the man who injures you and do not you yourself reply.[51]

The concept of justice, itself a part of *ma'at*, was also strong among people on all social levels. In a well-known Middle Kingdom document, *The Eloquent Peasant*, the poor but very wise character named in the title of the work proclaims, "Speak justice! Do justice! For it is powerful, it is far-reaching, [and] it endures. All that devotion to it shall discover leads on to honor and to veneration."[52] Such attitudes and ideas made antisocial and criminal behavior particularly abhorrent in the view of most people. And it helped to set the tone for the judgment and punishment of any transgressors.

Police: To Protect as Well as Punish

The phrase "do not you yourself reply" in the above passage by Amenemope emphasizes that society did not expect average citizens to respond on their own to wrongs perpetrated against them. Rather, it was expected that the authorities would round up wrongdoers, hear complaints, mete out justice, and deal with those found guilty of crimes. The first responders, so to speak, among these "authorities" were the police. The Egyptians seem to have had a strikingly modern view of their role—namely

to protect society as well as to catch and punish criminals. This may have derived from the extensive air of civility and corresponding aversion to wrongdoing among the general populace. As Rosalie David puts it:

> Egyptian society was essentially law abiding and the police were not regarded as an unduly aggressive force. Their duty as guardians and protectors was at least as important as their

The concept of ma'at *was sometimes personified as a goddess, as in this painted relief.*

Justice Pleases the Gods

The Middle Kingdom document known as The Eloquent Peasant *(translated in John L. Foster's collection of Egyptian literature) makes the point that people should always treat their fellows justly, first and foremost because it is the will of the gods and therefore is morally right.*

Do justice for the Lord of Justice [the god Osiris, who oversees the final judgment of people's souls in the afterlife], who is the wise perfection of his justice. Reed pen, papyrus, and palette of Thoth [god of knowledge and writing] all dread to write injustice. When good is truly good, that good is priceless. But justice is forever, and down to the very grave it goes with one who does it. His burial conceals that man within the ground, yet his good name shall never perish from the earth. The memory of him becomes a precious thing. He is a standard written in the word of God.

Osiris, Lord of Justice (sitting on the throne at right), passes judgment on two petitioners.

punitive role. . . . The police force . . . existed to uphold the established order as handed down by the gods and to protect the weak against the strong.[53]

Regarding the policemen themselves, Egypt did not have full-time local police officers paid by local taxpayers, as in modern countries. Instead, the police seem to have been individuals appointed and paid by central or local government officials. There were two general types of police-men—those who guarded and patrolled, and those who inflicted punishment. Of the first group—the guardians—some patrolled the rural farming and desert areas to keep desert nomads and outlaws from harassing the farmers and other peasants. These guardians were a fairly common fixture in Egyptian society at least as early as the Middle Kingdom and probably considerably earlier.

During the New Kingdom the role of police guardians expanded further, as it became common for the government to hire mercenary (paid) soldiers for this duty. Fighters called Medjay, from Nubia (the African region directly south of Egypt), were recruited to guard palaces, temples, and cemeteries (to make sure no one disturbed tombs, which often held collections of valuables). Some of these police became quite specialized, as in the case of those called *s'sha*, who kept watch over the pharaoh's harem.

The Medjay also guarded the villages and work sites of the craftsmen and laborers who built royal and wealthy tombs. Surviving records from Deir el-Medina show that at least eight policemen were assigned to watch over the village. However, they did not live in the town itself. For reasons that are unclear, their houses were located in a separate area nearby. This may have been done to keep them independent and aloof, so that they would remain impartial in legal cases involving members of the community.

In keeping with the dual role of Egyptian policemen, some enforced societal and community rules and standards. They could and often did enforce tax collection, for example. And they had the authority to use threats and even minor beatings to make sure that people complied. If a suspected or accused criminal or a slave ran away, they tracked him or her down and brought the person back to face justice. In

A master beats his slave. Sometimes such punishments were meted out by Medjay, policemen recruited from Nubia by the government.

such cases the police may have had plenty of help. Some evidence suggests that most average Egyptians viewed it as their civic duty to aid authorities in apprehending criminals. It is unclear whether they could make citizens' arrests. But a few surviving passages, like the following one (from *The Eloquent Peasant*), seem to show active involvement in crime prevention: "The one who stops a thief aids the officials. Do whatever shall oppose injustice. The refuge of the hard-pressed man, it is those same officials. Do whatever shall oppose deceit."[54]

The Medjay had other duties as well. They interrogated thieves and other petty criminals, for instance, and inflicted punishments on those found guilty in court. Their other functions, as Rosalie David points out, included

> inspecting tombs, acting as witnesses [in court and other settings], and bringing messages and official letters. Sometimes they were asked to help the official workforce [that erected public structures] and assist with the transport of stone blocks.[55]

Local Courts and Judges

Once an accused criminal was apprehended or a citizen brought a complaint to the authorities, the courts and judges got involved. Again, ancient Egypt did not have a formal, complex system of courthouses, professional lawyers and judges, and so forth. So the word *courts* is used loosely to describe the general processes by which legal issues were decided and accused criminals found guilty or innocent. The exact people and procedures involved remain a bit unclear. This is partly because, as a matter of custom, most local crimes and trials and their outcomes were not recorded for posterity. Crimes against or involving the government *were* recorded (on ostraka or papyrus) and stored in temples or other official buildings. However, the vast majority of these records have not survived.

Based on the evidence that *has* survived, it appears that a legal or criminal case could be brought into one of three kinds of court settings. The first was on the local level. A local court, or *kenbet*, consisted of a group of magistrates (community leaders, officials, or elders), called *seru*. When necessity dictated, they got together to act as judges in criminal and civil cases. The panel of judges also sometimes included a policeman and/or a person representing the office of the pharaoh's chief administrator, the vizier. Thus, the Egyptians did not differentiate between the administrative and legal functions of their public officials. Any person in a position of authority might make legal judgments at one time or another. It is unknown whether the judges on a panel had to be unanimous to reach a verdict or convict an accused person.

Very little is known about the procedure in these informal hearings. The litigants (accuser and accused) did not have lawyers; instead, they presented the evidence of their cases themselves to the best of their ability. It appears that all (or at least most) of the evidence presented was oral. The fact that written documents were seldom if ever introduced as evidence may reflect the fact that the vast majority of people were illiterate and did not create or keep documents. The judges sometimes questioned the litigants. And at times they allowed witnesses to step forward and support or refute a litigant's claims. The judges also might go to the scene of a crime—a tomb, house, temple, or whatever—and conduct their own investigation. In general, in the absence of strict fixed rules, local courts seem to have been quite flexible in handling cases.

The Case of the Chisel Thief

Some of the particulars of a case brought to a local court at Deir el-Medina during the New Kingdom have survived and give some idea of the ancient Egyptian legal system in action. A workman named Neb-nefer registered a complaint that a woman named Herya had stolen his chisel. (In that place and time, a metal chisel was a fairly expensive item, so its theft was not seen as a trivial matter.) "I buried a chisel of mine in my house after the war, and it was stolen," Neb-nefer stated. He went on to explain that he had already done his own investigation by canvassing the village. "I made everyone . . . swear [by the gods] to his innocence regarding my chisel." One of these people, a woman named Nub-em-nehem, turned out to be an eyewitness to the theft. Neb-nefer recalled, "The lady Nub-em-nehem came to say to me: 'I saw Herya taking your chisel.'"[56]

The next step was to question the accused, Herya. "Are you indeed the one

Always Be Honest in Court

The New Kingdom document known as the Instruction of Amenemope, *which was intended to set down the characteristics, values, and actions of the ideal good person, gives the following advice to people who are scheduled to appear in court.*

Do not go to court before a [judge or other justice] official in order to falsify your words. Do not vacillate [hesitate] in your answers when your witnesses accuse. . . . Tell the truth before the official, lest he lay a hand on you [to punish you for lying]. . . . Do not confound [cause trouble for] a man in the law court in order to brush aside one who is right. . . . Do not make for yourself false documents; they are [a] deadly [form of] provocation. . . . Don't use for yourself the might [powers and privileges] of the gods, as if there were no Fate or Destiny [that will punish you for your wrongdoing in the final reckoning].

who stole this chisel of Neb-nefer, or not?" one of the judges asked her. The woman answered, "No! I am not the one who stole it."[57] But the judges pressed her, demanding that she swear her innocence before the gods. This was often an effective way to elicit the truth because most Egyptians were deeply religious and feared that swearing false oaths before a god might result in their being excluded from enjoying the afterlife. Nevertheless, Herya continued to deny her involvement in the theft.

The surviving account of the case then becomes somewhat vague. It says that "an hour later the court examined her." It is difficult to understand what the word *examine* means in this context. It is possible that it referred to interrogation using coercive means, including torture. However, no specific references to torture

Some courts were run by royal officials. This stela depicts an official named Ipepi.

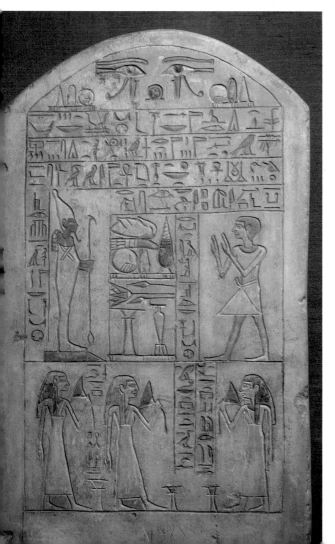

in Egyptian legal cases have ever been found. The "examination" may instead have consisted of a thorough investigation of Herya's house. The account goes on to say, "The servant Pa-shed [a scribe acting as a court officer as well as a judge] was sent out with her and she brought [back] the chisel. It was buried in her possession [i.e., on her property]."[58] This could mean that Pa-shed led the on-site search, discovered the chisel, and forced the accused to bring it back to the court. The main difference between this case and most modern theft cases is that the victim and the court did all the detective work that led to the conviction; the police seem to have played no role (although they did get involved in other cases).

Other Kinds of Courts

Another interesting development in the case against Herya was that the chisel was not the only item she had stolen. Found in the same hiding place with the chisel was a copper statue of a god she had filched from a temple. This was a much more serious crime than petty theft. As the court stated, "The theft of copper from here is the abomination [terrible offense] of this village."[59] The more heinous crime also did not fall under the jurisdiction (authority and control) of the local court, so Herya now found herself facing the second kind of ancient Egyptian court. This was the one connected with the office of the vizier, who handled cases involving major crimes. (As a very rough analogy, one might consider the difference between lower courts and the Supreme Court in the United States.)

The vizier had his own court officers, who were likely mostly scribes like Pa-shed since they were literate and able to keep careful records of investigations and trials. In the case of Herya, the vizier sent a scribe named Hat-iay to oversee her prosecution for stealing the statue. Hat-iay's interrogation of the accused took place "on the riverbank," an ominous reference mentioned in numerous other surviving legal accounts. It is unclear whether the river (more specifically water) had anything to do with the questioning; if so, it might have involved dunking the accused in the water over and over until she confessed. However, in Herya's case, there was no need for a confession since the stolen statue had already been found in her possession. "On the riverbank" might therefore have been a descriptive expression left over from a more ancient era in which people accused of crimes *had* been dunked to persuade them to confess. In any case, the vizier's court found Herya guilty. The court urged the vizier, "Let this woman who stole the chisel and also the [copper statue] be punished, so that no other woman in her position will do the same again!"[60]

The third kind of court in Egypt was oracular, or one that involved oracles, supernatural connections to the gods. (Oracular courts may not have become common until the Late Period.) It was thought that under certain conditions a god might communicate with humans, usually through some kind of movement of a statue of that deity. So the authorities sometimes asked a god to intervene and reveal the identity of a thief. Priests placed a god's image on a litter and carried the litter on their shoulders in a solemn procession. When a person asked the god a question, the priests and litter moved. A backward move indicated "no," while a move forward meant "yes." Modern scholars are unsure whether the priests consciously manipulated the oracle. Some suggest that the litter bearers actually believed that the god was directing them to move either backward or forward. Even if this was true much of the time, the opportunity for corruption and abuse was ever present. Certainly this was the most subjective and unreliable form of court trial conducted in ancient Egypt, at least by modern standards.

Punishments

After a court found an accused suspect guilty, punishment of some kind usually followed. In general, penalties were harsh compared to most of those administered in modern Western nations. Today, for instance, a person convicted of failing to pay his or her taxes or cheating on them pays a fine or, in a few exceptional cases, goes to jail for a few months. In ancient Egypt, by contrast, tax shirkers and cheats were forced to lie flat on the ground and endure a severe beating (as many as a hundred or more blows) with a whip or a stick. Repeated offenders might find themselves condemned to months or years of back-breaking forced labor in mines or quarries.

Surviving legal documents from Egypt mention a number of other punishments, some of them even more brutal. A male adulterer could receive up to a thousand blows with a whip or a stick, for example, while a female adulterer might have her nose cut off. And a man who raped a free-born woman was castrated. (Presumably raping a slave was not viewed as a crime, probably because slaves were, in legal terms, only pieces of property.) If a government official was caught skimming valuables from the treasury, he suffered the loss of his hands; a soldier who revealed a military secret had his tongue cut out; and prisoners who attempted to escape had their ears and noses amputated. Even more gruesome was the fate of a child who killed his or her parents. The penalty described in one account included placing the child on a bed of thorns for some undetermined length of time and then burning him or her to death.

It is uncertain, however, whether such extreme penalties were always inflicted for these crimes. The punishments described in these accounts may have been the maximum sentences for said offenses, and mitigating circumstances may have allowed for less severe penalties. Also, the surviving accounts do not always explain which punishments were meted out for which crimes. And there is the possibility that judges exercised considerable flexibility in imposing penalties. In other words, as a matter of custom a judge or panel of judges in one location may have called for a certain punishment for a certain crime; yet a

Beatings, like that depicted in this modern drawing based on an ancient painting, were likely the most common form of punishment.

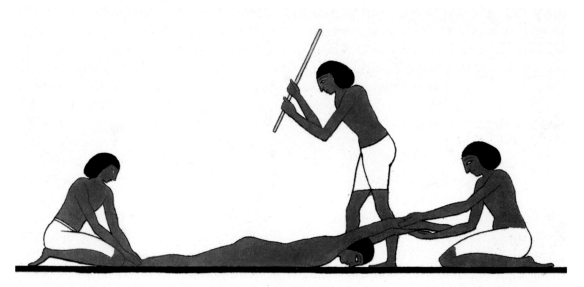

Farmers who failed to meet certain quotas set by the government were subject to the same kinds of beatings as ordinary criminals.

judge or panel of judges somewhere else might have imposed a different punishment for the same offense.

In general, it seems safe to conclude that minor crimes resulted in punishments such as beatings, forced labor, imprisonment, or exile. (In cases involving the last two, the convicted person's family could be incarcerated or banished along with him or her.) More serious crimes carried sentences such as disfigurement and death. When execution was imposed, as in the case of tomb robbing, one common method was to feed the condemned to crocodiles. (Owing to their privileged social positions, high-placed nobles and government officials sentenced to death were allowed to commit suicide rather than face being eaten alive.) As near as modern scholars can tell, however, capital punish-

ment was fairly rare. "The operating principle here," Rosalie David suggests, "was that disgrace could often be worse than death. Also, a rehabilitated person could be useful again to society, whereas an executed criminal could never contribute."[61]

If this was indeed the case, it shows that, despite the brutal nature of some criminal penalties, justice, and not personal or societal vengeance, was the primary goal of Egypt's legal system. The so-called eloquent peasant, famous for his wise sayings on legal matters, summed up the importance the Egyptians placed on the fair treatment of all people accused of wrongdoing: "Justice is forever, and down to the very grave it goes with one who does it. His burial conceals that [just] man within the ground, yet his good name shall never perish from the earth."[62]

Chapter Seven

Keeping Society Running: Occupations and Workers

Nearly all ancient Egyptians performed some kind of work on a regular basis. Some modern studies attempt to separate "professionals" from "ordinary workers" or to impose some other kind of classification of jobs based on the prestige, monetary rewards, or social status of those who performed them. But this approach often reflects the biases of the modern writers who pen such studies. It is probably fairer to the Egyptians themselves to view all the jobs they performed simply as occupations, each of which was essential in some way to keeping society running smoothly.

Thus, the farmer's role should not be discounted or glossed over simply because he was most often a poor peasant whose name has been lost in the mists of time. Although government administrators and scribes held prestigious and important positions, they could not have prospered without the food grown by the farmers. Nor could the architects have seen their buildings rise without the thousands of stonemasons and laborers who carried out their plans. Nor could the military generals whose names posterity preserved have earned their reputations without the countless soldiers who sweated, risked their lives, and sometimes died for them for minimal pay.

Speaking of pay, it should be emphasized that throughout most of Egypt's history all workers, whether of high or low status, were not paid in coins or paper money. Instead, all levels of the economy operated on the barter system—essentially the exchange of goods such as land, crops, livestock, slaves, and so forth, or the exchange of those goods for work performed. For their services, for example, high officials received rich estates from the pharaoh; and the officials and their families lived off of the considerable revenues produced by those estates. Similarly, construction workers and craftsmen most often received their wages in the form of bread and other foodstuffs, beer, vegetable oils, and clothing. (In the case of workers' villages like Deir el-Medina, the government also supplied their housing.)

In the early New Kingdom the government introduced a system in which all material goods had a certain value in gold, silver, or copper (for instance, X bushels of wheat would be equal in value to Y ounces of gold). But this was only to make payment of salaries and business transactions easier and fairer, and the barter system remained in place. Not until well into the Ptolemaic Period, after the Persians and Greeks had introduced coins into Egypt, did a true monetary system develop in the country.

Farmers

The fact that workers of all walks of life so often received foodstuffs for their salaries further illustrates the vital importance of farmers in Egyptian society. On a more basic level, because everyone, rich or poor, had to eat, the farming occupation was critical to maintaining normal standards of Egyptian life. And the farmers, in turn, were very much dependent on the Nile, without which they could not raise crops and perform their jobs.

Reconstructing certain aspects of the jobs performed by Egypt's peasant farmers is not overly difficult because various aspects of planting and harvesting appear in surviving tomb paintings. Also, many

This painting was found in the tomb of Mennah, a scribe under the pharaoh Thutmose IV. It shows farmers engaged in planting, harvesting, and other activities.

These harvesting scenes come from the tomb of a minor official named Sennedjem. In the upper panel, a farmer uses a sickle to cut wheat.

of the methods and practices they used survived into medieval and modern times in various parts of the Near East. In the planting phases, for instance, the farmers scattered their seeds by hand from sacks that hung from their necks and then employed simple wooden plows drawn by cattle or donkeys to work the seeds into the soil. Because the soil laid down by the yearly Nile floods was so rich and pliable, some farmers did not even need to plow. Rather, they simply allowed their goats, pigs, and other livestock to trample the seeds into the soil.

Following planting, the farmers' crops grew and matured until the spring harvest season. Lines of field workers (usually men because they generally had more upper-body strength than women) strode through the crops and swung wooden sickles to cut them down. Next, the family women and children gathered up the fallen crops and loaded them into wicker baskets. Then came the threshing process, in which the grain was separated from the stalks. During this work the farmworkers sang songs, including one praising Hapy, thought to be a divine spirit or force who guided the Nile's floods and thereby bestowed the gifts of food and prosperity on the people. "When sparkling he rises, the land stands rejoicing," one verse began.

Every belly is filled with elation, bones of the creatures are shaken by laughter, and teeth gleam, bared by welcoming smiles. Food-bringer, rich with provisions, himself the author of all good things, awe-striking master, yet sweet the [food] aromas rising about him . . . transforming the dust to pastures for cattle . . . filling the storerooms, heaping the grainsheds, giving his gifts to the poor. . . . Hapy, river spirit, may you flourish and return! Come back to Egypt bringing your benediction of peace, greening the banks of the Nile![63]

In addition to producing crops, Egyptian farmers performed many other chores and duties. A passage from a surviving document describes many of a typical farmer's daily duties and routines, which could be relentless and monotonous. It also mentions the hardship that could arise if the Nile's yearly flood failed to arrive. (It must be kept in mind that the passage was written by a scribe who was advising his pupils to become scribes, so it likely somewhat exaggerates the woes of farmers.)

[During] the inundation, he [the farmer] attends to his equipment. By day he cuts his farming tools; by night he twists his rope. Even his midday hour he spends on farm labor. . . . [When the inundation is over] the dried field lies before him. He goes out to get his team [of oxen or donkeys to pull the plow]. . . . He spends time cultivating [planting], and the snake is after him [to eat the seeds]. [Sometimes] it finishes off the seed as it falls to the ground. . . . [In those dreaded years when the inundation

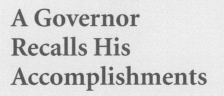

A Governor Recalls His Accomplishments

On occasion in ancient Egypt, commoners managed to rise to high positions in the bureaucracy or palace. One of these was Weni, who served under three Old Kingdom pharaohs. During the reign of Merenra (ca. 2287–2278 B.C.), Weni received his biggest promotion, as recalled in this passage from the latter's autobiography (quoted in volume 1 of Miriam Lichtheim's compilation of Egyptian literature), which also lists some of his duties and accomplishments.

When I was chamberlain of the palace and sandal-bearer, King Menenra . . . made me governor of Upper Egypt . . . because I was worthy in his majesty's heart. . . . I governed Upper Egypt for him in peace, so that no one attacked his fellow [i.e., did a good job of maintaining law and order]. I did every task. I counted everything that is countable [i.e., collected and recorded taxes levied on the locals] for the [official] residence in this Upper Egypt. . . . His majesty sent me to dig five [irrigation] canals . . . and to build three barges and four tow-boats. . . . I did it all in one year. Indeed, I made a saving for the palace [managed to come in under budget].

does not come and his fields go unwatered], he does not see a green blade [of wheat]. . . . His wife has gone down to the merchants and found nothing for barter. . . . There's no grain. If you have any sense, be a scribe [rather than a farmer].[64]

Government Administrators and Officials

Scribes were not so critical of government officials since those in positions of authority tended to be either scribes, former scribes themselves, or enjoyed lives free from menial labor, as scribes did. Most of those in such cushy bureaucratic jobs did not begin in poverty and work their way up the social and professional ladder. Instead, they acquired their high positions through fortunate accidents of birth and the pervasive custom of sons pursuing their fathers' professions. Indeed, most high officials were members of the nobility or priesthood.

There were occasional exceptions to this rule, however. One among them was a commoner named Weni, who rose through the ranks and served in a variety of important positions under three late Old Kingdom pharaohs (Teti, Pepi I, and Merenra). Among these positions were custodian of the storehouse, overseer of the royal robing room, senior official of the town of Nekhen (on the Nile south of Thebes), and eventually governor of Upper Egypt. (Upper Egypt was the southernmost section of the country and Lower Egypt the northernmost, as these directions were reckoned by the direction of the Nile's flow—south to north.)

Weni was probably not the most noteworthy administrator to serve in Egypt over the centuries. But he is important to modern observers because he left behind an autobiography in which he lists some of his duties. In the following passage, he recalls with pride how King Pepi trusted him so much that he allowed him to handle problems that developed within the highly private quarters of the royal harem:

> While I was senior warden of Nekhen, his majesty made me a sole companion [close adviser]. . . . I acted for his majesty's praise in guarding, escorting, and attending the king. I acted [appropriately] throughout [my tenure in the job], so that his majesty praised me for it exceedingly. When there was a secret charge in the royal harem against [the pharaoh's chief wife], his majesty made me go in to [take care of the matter] alone. No chief judge and vizier, no official was there; only I alone, because I was worthy, because I was rooted in his majesty's heart. . . . Never before had one like me heard a secret of the king's harem, but his majesty made me hear it because I was worthy . . . beyond any noble of his, beyond any servant of his.[65]

The positions Weni held were only a few among many in Egypt's national bureaucracy. The top administrator, of course, was the vizier (*tjaty*), usually a former scribe. He directly advised the king and, with the help of numerous assistants (many of them also scribes), in general ran the national government. Other government administrators were in charge of foreign diplomacy; overseeing agriculture and grain storage; building and maintaining temples and tombs; running the prisons, mines, and quarries; collecting taxes; and so forth.

Soldiers

Government administrators were also in charge of supplying the army with food and other provisions. They dealt directly with members of one of Egypt's oldest and most important occupations—soldiering.

It appears that a large percentage of soldiers entered the profession the same way that people in most other professions did, namely following in their fathers' footsteps. When a man joined the army, his name was recorded on lists that were maintained from one generation to the next. And when he retired or died in the line of duty, his son took his place. The son inherited not only the position but also all the benefits his father had earned, including the use of a small piece of land owned by the government (more technically the pharaoh, who in theory owned all the land in Egypt). Soldiers did not gain the right to own such land plots themselves until late in the New Kingdom.

These painted wooden figures of soldiers date from the Middle Kingdom. While on duty, soldiers often lived in squalid conditions.

A Soldier's Hardships

The document modern scholars call the Lansing Papyrus contains a long tract in which a scribe describes the hardships of most common professions in order to persuade his students to avoid these occupations and become scribes instead. This passage (translated in volume 2 of Miriam Lichtheim's collection of Egyptian literature) focuses on the drawbacks of soldiering.

Let me tell you the woes of the soldier. . . . He is awakened at any hour [of the day or night]. . . . He toils until the Sun sets in the darkness of night. He is hungry [and] his belly hurts. He is dead while yet alive. When he receives the grain ration . . . it is not good for grinding. . . . [He often has] no clothes, no sandals. [When on campaign] his march is uphill through moun-

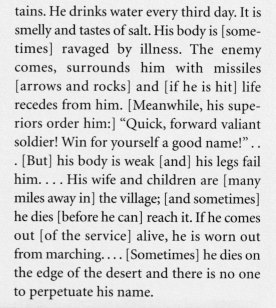

tains. He drinks water every third day. It is smelly and tastes of salt. His body is [sometimes] ravaged by illness. The enemy comes, surrounds him with missiles [arrows and rocks] and [if he is hit] life recedes from him. [Meanwhile, his superiors order him:] "Quick, forward valiant soldier! Win for yourself a good name!" . . . [But] his body is weak [and] his legs fail him. . . . His wife and children are [many miles away in] the village; [and sometimes] he dies [before he can] reach it. If he comes out [of the service] alive, he is worn out from marching. . . . [Sometimes] he dies on the edge of the desert and there is no one to perpetuate his name.

A New Kingdom painting shows military recruits receiving a lecture and getting haircuts.

In addition to government grants of land on retirement, soldiers were lured into the profession by the opportunity to acquire booty. After capturing an enemy camp or town, the victorious pharaoh (or his general) usually came into the possession of a good deal of gold, jewels, fine fabrics, horses, slaves, and other valuables. And following custom, he usually shared some of the captured treasure with his troops. Another common custom was for commanders to allow a soldier to keep as slaves any prisoners he had personally captured. Still another perk of the soldiering profession was marching in the pharaoh's victory parade in front of thousands of cheering countrymen. Finally, a valiant soldier who proved himself in battle might receive medals and other decorations not unlike those awarded to outstanding modern soldiers. In this regard, the surviving autobiography of a soldier named Ahmose, who lived in the early New Kingdom, is valuable and revealing. The author describes the medals, slaves, and lands he received from the government for his military service as well as the circumstances of that service:

> I speak to you . . . that I may let you know the favors which have come to me. I have been awarded gold [medals for bravery] seven times . . . and [have been given] male and female slaves in like manner, and I have been vested with very many fields [to farm]. The reputation of a valiant man is from what he has done. . . . I had my upbringing in the town of el-Kab, my father being a soldier of the King. . . . Then I served as [a] soldier in his place in the ship [named] "The Wild Bull" . . . when I was still a boy . . . while I was still sleeping in a net hammock. But after I had set up a household [and taken a wife?], then I was taken on the ship "Northern," because I was valiant. Thus, I used to accompany the King . . . on foot, following his excursions in his chariot. When the town of Avaris was besieged [during the campaign in which the Egyptians expelled the Hyksos invaders], then I showed valor on foot in the presence of his majesty. . . . Then the very prestigious medal [known as] the Gold of Valor was given to me.[66]

On the other hand, everyday life for most soldiers, especially on campaigns, could be very difficult. Typical were long marches through barren regions; extended periods living in squalid conditions far from home and family; numerous camp duties, including large doses of backbreaking work; the increased chance of catching various diseases; and harsh discipline. Quite a few writings warned young men about the rigors of military life, including one that said that a soldier could be "awakened at any hour" of the day or night and often toiled "until the Sun set in the darkness of night." Military food was sometimes poor and in short supply, so "he is hungry [and] his belly hurts." Only rarely, if at all, during his hitch did he see his wife and children. And if he managed to make it home alive at the end of his service, his

Painted wooden figures depict potters at work. The man on the right makes a pot, while the man on the left fires finished pots in an open-fire kiln.

body and spirit were exhausted from his long exertions. The following excerpts from the same document, like those describing the woes of farmers, were intended to encourage young men to be scribes rather than soldiers. So they likely exaggerate the drawbacks of soldiering a bit. However, they do accurately describe many of the common hazards of military campaigning in the ancient world.

Let me tell you the woes of the soldier.... [Because of limited supplies] he drinks water [only] every third day. It is smelly and tastes of salt. His body is [sometimes] ravaged by illness. The enemy comes, surrounds him with missiles [arrows and rocks] and [if hit] life recedes from him. . . . [Sometimes] he dies [before he can finish his hitch and return home]. If he comes out [of the service] alive, he is worn out from marching. . . . If he leaps [runs away] and joins the deserters, all his people [family members] are imprisoned. . . . Be a scribe and be spared from soldiering![67]

A Host of Other Occupations

Although large numbers of Egyptian men served as soldiers, even more worked in a host of other trades and occupations that helped maintain the general standard of living in the country. Some of these occupations are only briefly described in the surviving sources. But at least they confirm that these jobs existed and give some indication of how they were practiced.

Barbers constitute an example. Today, people are used to seeing barbers ply their trade in shops to which patrons go when need dictates. The same was true in ancient Rome. In Egypt, as in medieval Europe, however, most barbers were itinerants who traveled around looking for customers. According to *The Satire of Trades*, "The barber [works] far into the evening . . . [taking] himself from street to street to hunt down any who are ripe for barbering."[68]

The same document describes potters, although it does so in derogatory terms since the author believed that the profession of scribe was the only decent one. "The potter with his earth and clay," it begins,

rises early with the servants. Weeds and swine hinder his efforts until he manages to fire his pots. His clothing is stiff with slime [from the wet clay] and his leather apron is in tatters. The air which enters up

his nose spews directly from his kiln. He makes a pestle of his feet to stamp the clay down flat.[69]

The author's bias and exaggerations aside, the passage at least confirms that potters fired their products in ovens, that they wore leather aprons, and that trampling with the feet was a common method they used to prepare the clay.

Potters were among the many craftsmen and laborers in Egypt who performed jobs that members of the upper classes often

Female entertainers appear in this early New Kingdom painting.

Tears of the Washerman

This excerpt from the well-known Middle Kingdom document popularly known as The Satire of Trades *(quoted in John L. Foster's* Ancient Egyptian Literature*) employs a sarcastic tone to emphasize the negative aspects of the occupation of "washerman" (launderer, almost always a male profession in ancient Egypt).*

The washerman washing on the riverbank bows low in the presence of the crocodile god. . . . Oh, there is no profession [that] satisfies like this, distinguished above any other calling! He [the washerman] kneads [handles and squeezes] all sorts of excrement [filth and crap], with not a limb of him left clean. He does the undergarments of a woman full of the stains of her menstruation. Tears are his daylong at the hot washing bowls or as he heaves the pounding stone [a stone mallet used to beat the clothes, thereby loosening up the dirt]. The tub of dirty water whispers, "Come to me and let me overflow because of you!"

looked down on. Included, along with farmers, were miners, quarrymen, construction workers, carpenters, stonemasons, metalsmiths, most merchants, leatherworkers, launderers, cloth and clothes makers, and fishermen, to name only a few. To this list can be added all manner of servants, whether free or unfree.

Women Workers

A great deal has been written about these occupations in various modern books and articles. One that has often been neglected is that of female workers, partly because the evidence for their lives and work is rather scarce. It has been established that women sometimes made livings by spinning and weaving, assisting bakers, sowing and harvesting crops, hairdressing, acting as wet nurses, and entertaining (singing and dancing).

Evidence for women entertainers comes mainly from tomb and palace wall paintings. Some show upper-class women entertaining their husbands and friends, which means that they did not make their livings this way. But troupes of paid singers and dancers from outside the household are also frequently in evidence. "Such troupes," Gay Robins points out, "could be attached to religious institutions, and royal and private households." In other words, rich people sometimes hired such entertainers on a full- or part-time basis. Furthermore, women were not simply singers and dancers in these troupes but for a while also managed them. "In the Old Kingdom," Robins continues, "it was possible for a woman to be an overseer of one of these troupes, [although] by the Middle Kingdom this position of authority had passed to men."[70]

Female hairdressers also generally worked in well-to-do households since the poor clearly could not afford their services. And nearly all of the other servants attending the women of rich households were women. Scholars have identified about twenty kinds of female servants during the Middle Kingdom, although almost nothing is known about their lives and duties. One of these servile positions, for example, bore the title of sealer, a job also performed by men. At least eight references to women sealers are known from the Old Kingdom alone. It is presumed that their jobs consisted of applying seals, wads of wax stamped with a name or some other sign identifying the owner of some kind of property. The Egyptians did not have locks to safeguard chests or rooms. So they applied wax seals to the edges of box lids and doors, knowing that thieves had to break the seals to get in. (The owner periodically checked the seal to confirm that nothing was amiss.)

A Universal Truth

It is unfortunate for modern observers of ancient Egypt that so little concrete, detailed information about many of the common occupations of that land has survived. Part of the problem is that so few Egyptians could read and write and none of those who were literate considered recording such details for the benefit of people in diverse future civilizations. After all, there seemed no need to do so. At the time virtually all Egyptians assumed (as many people mistakenly do today) that their civilization would continue largely unchanged forever. Nevertheless, a tiny handful of literate individuals at least recognized the universal truth that written literature could and would outlast many human generations and make at least some aspects of the long-dead past immortal. One far-thinking New Kingdom scribe stated it this way:

> Man decays. His corpse is dust, and all of his kin have perished. But a book makes him remembered. . . . Better is a book than a well-built house. . . . Nearly every person who has lived before has been forgotten, but those who wrote books and those they wrote [about]—their names have become everlasting![71]

Notes

Introduction: The Ancient Egyptians Enjoyed Life

1. James F. Romano, *Daily Life of the Ancient Egyptians*. Pittsburgh: Carnegie Museum of Natural History, 1990, p. 49.
2. Quoted in Miriam Lichtheim, ed., *Ancient Egyptian Literature: A Book of Readings*, vol. 1. Berkeley and Los Angeles: University of California Press, 1975–1976, p. 66.
3. Quoted in John L. Foster, trans., *Ancient Egyptian Literature*. Austin: University of Texas Press, 2001, pp. 179–80.
4. Romano, *Daily Life of the Ancient Egyptians*, p. 38.
5. Gay Robins, *Women of Ancient Egypt*. Cambridge, MA: Harvard University Press, 1993, p. 14.
6. Quoted in Lichtheim, *Ancient Egyptian Literature*, vol. 1, p. 68.
7. Quoted in Foster, *Ancient Egyptian Literature*, p. 24.
8. Quoted in Foster, *Ancient Egyptian Literature*, p. 226.

Chapter 1: The Focus of Life: Home and Family

9. Herodotus, *The Histories*, trans. Aubrey de Sélincourt. New York: Penguin, 1972, pp. 142–43.
10. Herodotus, *Histories*, p. 143.
11. Robins, *Women of Ancient Egypt*, p. 99.
12. Quoted in Lichtheim, *Ancient Egyptian Literature*, vol. 2, p. 136.
13. Quoted in Lichtheim, *Ancient Egyptian Literature*, vol. 1, pp. 66–67.

Chapter 2: Women vs. Men: Love, Marriage, and Divorce

14. Quoted in Lichtheim, *Ancient Egyptian Literature*, vol. 1, p. 69.
15. Eugen Strouhal, *Life of the Ancient Egyptians*. Norman: University of Oklahoma Press, 1992, p. 57.
16. Quoted in Foster, *Ancient Egyptian Literature*, p. 19. It is important to emphasize that, despite the female perspective, this passage was probably not composed by a woman. No substantive female writers are known from the Old, Middle, and New kingdoms.
17. Quoted in Foster, *Ancient Egyptian Literature*, p. 90.
18. Quoted in Lichtheim, *Ancient Egyptian Literature*, vol. 2, p. 136.
19. Quoted in Lichtheim, *Ancient Egyptian Literature*, vol. 2, p. 143.
20. Quoted in Lichtheim, *Ancient Egyptian Literature*, vol. 2, p. 137.

21. Quoted in Alan H. Gardiner and Kurt Sethe, *Egyptian Letters to the Dead*. London: Egypt Exploration Society, 1928, pp. 8–9.
22. Quoted in A.G. McDowell, Village *Life in Ancient Egypt*. New York: Oxford University Press, 1999, pp. 34–35.
23. Quoted in McDowell, *Village Life in Ancient Egypt*, pp. 45–46.
24. Romano, *Daily Life of the Ancient Egyptians*, pp. 5, 8.

Chapter 3: Personal Care: Dress, Grooming, and Health

25. Herodotus, *Histories*, p. 143.
26. Robins, *Women of Ancient Egypt*, p. 181.
27. Strouhal, *Life of the Ancient Egyptians*, pp. 72–74.
28. Herodotus, *Histories*, p. 134.
29. Quoted in Josephine Mayer and Tom Prideaux, eds., *Never to Die: The Egyptians in Their Own Words*. New York: Viking, 1938, p. 77.
30. Quoted in Mayer and Prideaux, *Never to Die*, p. 80.
31. Quoted in Mayer and Prideaux, *Never to Die*, p. 79.
32. Quoted in Mayer and Prideaux, *Never to Die*, p. 79.
33. Quoted in Mayer and Prideaux, *Never to Die*, p. 51.

Chapter 4: The World's Breadbasket: Foods and Diet

34. Romano, *Daily Life of the Ancient Egyptians*, pp. 35–36.

35. Romano, *Daily Life of the Ancient Egyptians*, pp. 32–33.
36. Strouhal, *Life of the Ancient Egyptians*, pp. 127–28.
37. Quoted in Strouhal, *Life of the Ancient Egyptians*, p. 133.
38. Quoted in Lichtheim, *Ancient Egyptian Literature*, vol. 1, p. 137.

Chapter 5: In the Wise Man's Footsteps: Education and Learning

39. T.G.H. James, *Pharaoh's People: Scenes from Life in Imperial Egypt*. New York: Tauris Parke, 2003, pp. 136–37.
40. Strouhal, *Life of the Ancient Egyptians*, p. 31.
41. A. Rosalie David, *Handbook to Life in Ancient Egypt*. New York: Facts On File, 1998, p. 137.
42. David, *Handbook to Life in Ancient Egypt*, p. 204.
43. Quoted in Foster, *Ancient Egyptian Literature*, pp. 33–34.
44. Quoted in Alan H. Gardiner, *Late-Egyptian Miscellanies*. Brussels, Belgium: Reine Elizabeth Egyptian Foundation, 1937, p. 68.
45. Quoted in Gardiner, *Late-Egyptian Miscellanies*, pp. 24, 85.
46. David, *Handbook to Life in Ancient Egypt*, p. 207.
47. Quoted in Lichtheim, *Ancient Egyptian Literature*, vol. 1, pp. 63–64.
48. Quoted in W.K. Simpson, ed., *The Literature of Ancient Egypt: An*

Anthology of Stories, Instructions, and Poetry. New Haven, CT: Yale University Press, 1973, pp. 244, 253, 254–55, 262.

49. Strouhal, *Life of the Ancient Egyptians,* pp. 33–34.

Chapter 6: Maintaining *Ma'at:* Crime and Punishment

50. Ian Shaw and Paul Nicholson, *The Dictionary of Ancient Egypt.* New York: Harry N. Abrams, 1995, p. 159.
51. Quoted in Foster, *Ancient Egyptian Literature,* p. 209.
52. Quoted in Foster, *Ancient Egyptian Literature,* p. 185.
53. David, *Handbook to Life in Ancient Egypt,* pp. 231–32.
54. Quoted in Foster, *Ancient Egyptian Literature,* p. 184.
55. David, *Handbook to Life in Ancient Egypt,* p. 232.
56. Quoted in McDowell, *Village Life in Ancient Egypt,* p. 187.
57. Quoted in McDowell, *Village Life in Ancient Egypt,* p. 187.
58. Quoted in McDowell, *Village Life in Ancient Egypt,* p. 188.
59. Quoted in McDowell, *Village Life in Ancient Egypt,* p. 188.
60. Quoted in McDowell, *Village Life in Ancient Egypt,* p. 188.
61. David, *Handbook to Life in Ancient Egypt,* p. 94.
62. Quoted in Foster, *Ancient Egyptian Literature,* p. 185.

Chapter 7: Keeping Society Running: Occupations and Workers

63. Quoted in Foster, *Ancient Egyptian Literature,* pp. 111–12, 117.
64. Quoted in Lichtheim, *Ancient Egyptian Literature,* vol. 2, p. 170.
65. Quoted in Lichtheim, *Ancient Egyptian Literature,* vol. 1, p. 19.
66. Quoted in James B. Pritchard, ed., *Ancient Near Eastern Texts Relating to the Old Testament.* Princeton, NJ: Princeton University Press, 1969, p. 233.
67. Quoted in Lichtheim, *Ancient Egyptian Literature,* vol. 2, p. 172.
68. Quoted in Foster, *Ancient Egyptian Literature,* p. 35.
69. Quoted in Foster, *Ancient Egyptian Literature,* p. 35.
70. Robins, *Women of Ancient Egypt,* p. 120.
71. Quoted in Lichtheim, *Ancient Egyptian Literature,* vol. 2, pp. 176–77.

Chronology

General Time Periods of Ancient Egypt (as formulated by modern scholars)

B.C.

ca. 9000–5500
Approximate years of Egypt's Neolithic Age (or New Stone Age), before the advent of towns and states, during which tools and weapons were made exclusively from stone.

ca. 5500–3100
Years of Egypt's so-called Predynastic Period, during which the country is divided into many small city-states and eventually into two major kingdoms— Upper Egypt and Lower Egypt.

ca. 3100–2686
Years of the Early Dynastic Period, encompassing the reigns of the nine rulers of the First Dynasty and seven rulers of the Second Dynasty.

ca. 2686–2181
Years of the Old Kingdom (encompassing the rulers of the Third, Fourth, Fifth, and Sixth dynasties), during which most of Egypt's pyramids are built, including the largest ones, at Giza (near modern Cairo).

ca. 2181–2055
Years of the First Intermediate Period, which witnessed much civil strife and a partial breakdown of central authority and law and order.

ca. 2055–1650
Years of the Middle Kingdom (encompassing the Eleventh, Twelfth, Thirteenth, and Fourteenth dynasties), in which the Egyptians begin expanding their territory by conquest and their wealth through trade.

ca. 1650–1550
Years of the Second Intermediate Period, also called the Hyksos Period in reference to an Asiatic people of that name who invaded and occupied Egypt.

ca. 1550–1069
Years of the New Kingdom (encompassing the Eighteenth, Nineteenth, and Twentieth dynasties), in which a series of vigorous pharaohs create an Egyptian empire and erect numerous large temples, palaces, and forts.

ca. 1069–747
Years of the Third Intermediate Period, in which Egypt falls into steady military, political, and cultural decline.

ca. 747–332
Years of the Late Period, during most of which members of non-Egyptian dynasties rule Egypt.

332–323
Years in which the Greek Macedonian

conqueror Alexander the Great rules Egypt.

323–30
Years of the Ptolemaic Period (or Egypt's Greek Period), during which Alexander's

general Ptolemy and his descendants rule Egypt.

30 B.C.–A.D. 395
Years of the Roman Period, in which a series of Roman emperors control Egypt.

Glossary

adj: Animal fats, frequently used in cooking.

amulet: An object, either worn or carried, thought to have magical properties that would protect the owner.

antiquity: Ancient times.

bener: Date juice, which Egyptians of average means used to sweeten food.

brazier: A bowl-like container, often made of metal, used in ancient lands to burn charcoal for cooking and heating.

flax: A plant from which the ancient Egyptians derived fibers to make linen fabric for clothes.

himation: A cloaklike garment introduced into Egypt by the Greeks.

kenbet: Local courts or panels of judges.

khol: A black cosmetic eyeliner made by grinding up various lead compounds.

ma'at: A general term that embraced such concepts as "order," "justice," and "correctness."

Medjay: Nubian fighters employed by the Egyptian authorities as policemen.

merhet: Vegetable oils, frequently used in cooking.

natron (or natrum): A mineral salt the Egyptians used in the process of embalming and to rinse out their mouths on a daily basis.

nemes: A pleated headdress, covering the top of the forehead and flaring at the sides, that was worn by royalty in ancient Egypt.

ostraka (singular is ostrakon): Pieces of broken pottery or limestone often used to write on in the ancient world.

papyrus (plural is papyri): A water plant from which the Egyptians made a kind of paper.

relief (or bas-relief): A carving partly raised into three dimensions from a flat surface.

scarabs: Amulets or other pieces of jewelry shaped like scarab beetles.

scribes: Literate persons who often acted as teachers but also worked in various administrative, legal, and military capacities.

sebi: A ceremony undertaken by Egyptian males when they were about fourteen to mark the rite of passage from boyhood to manhood.

sen shem shem: "Cleansing of the mouth"; the common name for the daily cleanliness ritual of rinsing out the mouth with mineral salts.

seru: Local administrative officials who doubled as court judges.

stela (plural is **stelae**): A stone or wooden slab used as a marker or a monument and often inscribed with text, pictures, or both.

vizier (*tjaty*): A pharaoh's chief governmental administrator, who also oversaw the country's highest courts.

For Further Reading

Books

Lionel Casson, *Everyday Life in Ancient Egypt*. Baltimore: Johns Hopkins University Press, 2001. An excellent, fascinating examination of ancient Egyptian life by a great scholar. (The reading level is high school and general adult.)

Linda Honan, *Spend a Day in Ancient Egypt: Projects and Activities That Bring the Past to Life*. Hoboken, NJ: Wiley, 1999. A very informative and entertaining book that uses a hands-on approach to learning about ancient Egyptian life.

Joyce Milton and Charles Micucci, *Hieroglyphs*. New York: Grosset and Dunlap, 2000. This introduction to the picture-signs of ancient Egyptian writing is well organized and easy to read.

James F. Romano, *Daily Life of the Ancient Egyptians*. Pittsburgh: Carnegie Museum of Natural History, 1990. Not a children's book, but brief and clearly written enough to appeal to junior high schoolers and up.

Jane Shuter, *Builders and Craftsmen of Ancient Egypt*. Crystal Lake, IL: Heinemann Library, 1998. A well-written general examination of ancient Egyptian builders and artisans.

———, *Life in an Egyptian Workers' Village*. Crystal Lake, IL: Heinemann Library, 2004. Examines what life was like in the residential areas that were erected near the major construction sites in ancient Egypt.

Web Sites

Ancient Egyptian Papyrus (www.mnsu.edu/emuseum/prehistory/egypt/dailylife/papyrus.html). A brief overview of the making and use of ancient papyrus, the paper on which the Egyptians and other ancient people wrote literature.

Childhood in Ancient Egypt (http://nefertiti.iwebland.com/people/childhood.htm). Discusses the birth process, toddlers, education, and how families and society dealt with the death of a child.

The Discovery of the Tombs of the Pyramid Builders at Giza (www.guardians.net/hawass/buildtomb.htm). Renowned Egyptian archaeologist Zahi Hawass describes the recent discovery of a cemetery used by the workers who built the Giza pyramids.

Egyptian Clothing (http://nefertiti.iwebland.com/timelines/topics/clothing.htm). Discusses fabrics, styles of dress, laundering clothes, and footwear.

Egyptian Houses and Gardens (http://nefertiti.iwebland.com/timelines/topics/housing.htm). Provides information on townhouses and their layout, workers' houses, large estates, and the gardens found in and around these homes.

Law and Order in Ancient Egypt (http://nefertiti.iwebland.com/law_and_order/index.htm). Talks about crime, police and how they apprehended criminals, laws, judges, trials, and punishments.

Play in Ancient Egypt (http://nefertiti.iwebland.com/timelines/topics/games.htm). Discusses children's games, toys, and board games. This site is part of a larger and very useful collection of links about ancient Egyptian culture.

Works Consulted

Major Works

A. Rosalie David, *Handbook to Life in Ancient Egypt*. New York: Facts On File, 1998. A handy compilation of general information about ancient Egyptian society, customs, people, and ideas.

Sergio Donadoni, ed., *The Egyptians*. Trans. Robert Bianchi et al. Chicago: University of Chicago Press, 1990. This work contains a series of long essays by noted scholars, including informative ones on ancient Egyptian peasants, priests, slaves, craftsmen, and women.

Rosalind Hall, *Egyptian Textiles*. Princes Risborough, UK: Shire, 1990. An excellent introduction to ancient Egyptian fabrics and clothing.

T.G.H. James, *Pharaoh's People: Scenes from Life in Imperial Egypt*. New York: Tauris Parke, 2003. The author goes into considerable detail on aspects of ancient Egyptian society that normally receive less attention, including justice, literacy, and the domestic economy.

Jill Kamil, *The Ancient Egyptians: Life in the Old Kingdom*. Cairo: American University in Cairo Press, 1996. A thoughtful and useful overview of life in the Old Kingdom.

Gay Robins, *Women of Ancient Egypt*. Cambridge, MA: Harvard University Press, 1993. A noted scholar of ancient Egypt delivers a well-written, informative overview of the subject.

John Romer, *Ancient Lives: Daily Life in Egypt of the Pharaohs*. New York: Holt, Rinehart, and Winston, 1984. One of the best of many general studies of ancient Egyptian life.

David P. Silverman, ed., *Ancient Egypt*. New York: Oxford University Press, 1997. A very useful general depiction of ancient Egyptian culture, with sections on urban life, houses, gender roles, religion, and writing.

Eugen Strouhal, *Life of the Ancient Egyptians*. Norman: University of Oklahoma Press, 1992. One of the best recent general studies of ancient Egyptian life, with plenty of information on occupations, childhood and learning, houses, clothing and grooming, farming, the status and duties of women, and much more.

Other Important Works

Primary Sources

James H. Breasted, ed. and trans., *Ancient Records of Egypt*. 5 vols. New York: Russell and Russell, 1962.

——, ed. and trans., *The Edwin Smith Medical Papyrus*. 2 vols. Chicago: University of Chicago Press, 1930.

John L. Foster, trans., *Ancient Egyptian Literature*. Austin: University of Texas Press, 2001.

Alan H. Gardiner, *Late-Egyptian Miscellanies*. Brussels, Belgium: Reine Elizabeth Egyptian Foundation, 1937.

Alan H. Gardiner and Kurt Sethe, *Egyptian Letters to the Dead*. London: Egypt Exploration Society, 1928.

Herodotus, *The Histories*. Trans. Aubrey de Sélincourt. New York: Penguin, 1972.

Miriam Lichtheim, ed., *Ancient Egyptian Literature: A Book of Readings*. 2 vols. Berkeley and Los Angeles: University of California Press, 1975–1976.

Josephine Mayer and Tom Prideaux, eds., *Never to Die: The Egyptians in Their Own Words*. New York: Viking, 1938.

A.G. McDowell, *Village Life in Ancient Egypt*. New York: Oxford University Press, 1999.

Pliny the Elder, *Natural History*, excerpted in *Natural History: A Selection*. Trans. John F. Healy. New York: Penguin, 1991.

James B. Pritchard, ed., *Ancient Near Eastern Texts Relating to the Old Testament*. Princeton, NJ: Princeton University Press, 1969.

W.K. Simpson, ed., *The Literature of Ancient Egypt: An Anthology of Stories, Instructions, and Poetry*. New Haven, CT: Yale University Press, 1973.

Modern Sources

Paul G. Bahn, ed., *The Cambridge Illustrated History of Archaeology*. New York: Cambridge University Press, 1996.

Bob Brier, *Ancient Egyptian Magic*. New York: HarperCollins, 2001.

Karl W. Butzer, *Early Hydraulic Civilization in Egypt*. Chicago: University of Chicago Press, 1976.

Manfred Decker, *Sports and Games in Ancient Egypt*. New Haven, CT: Yale University Press, 1992.

Nicolas Grimal, *A History of Ancient Egypt*. Trans. Ian Shaw. Oxford, UK: Blackwell, 1992.

Alfred Lucas and J.R. Harris, *Ancient Egyptian Materials and Industries*. Mineola, NY: Dover, 1999.

Donald B. Redford, ed., *The Ancient Gods Speak: A Guide to Egyptian Religion*. New York: Oxford University Press, 2002.

Nicholas Reeves, *Ancient Egypt: The Great Discoveries*. New York: Thames and Hudson, 2000.

Ian Shaw and Paul Nicholson, *The Dictionary of Ancient Egypt*. New York: Harry N. Abrams, 1995.

Index

Picture Credits

About the Author

Historian and award-winning writer Don Nardo has written or edited numerous books about the ancient world, including *Empires of Mesopotamia, The Ancient Greeks, Life of a Roman Gladiator, The Etruscans, Ancient Civilizations,* and the *Greenhaven Encyclopedia of Greek and Roman Mythology.* Mr. Nardo lives with his wife, Christine, in Massachusetts.